EMPLOYEE BENEFITS FOR SMALL BUSINESS

MW00709427

JANE WHITE
and
BRUCE PYENSON

Prentice Hall

New York • London • Toronto • Sydney • Tokyo • Singapore

Second Edition

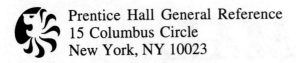 Prentice Hall General Reference
15 Columbus Circle
New York, NY 10023

A J.K. Lasser Book

J.K. Lasser, Prentice Hall, and colophons are
registered trademarks of Simon & Schuster, Inc.

Library of Congress Cataloging-in-Publication Data

White, Jane
    Employee benefits for small business / Jane White and Bruce
Pyenson.—2nd ed.
        p.   cm.
    "A J.K. Lasser book"—Verso t.p.
    Includes bibliographical references and index.
    ISBN 0-671-86676-1
        1. Employee fringe benefits—United States. 2. Small business—
United States—Personnel management. 3. Insurance, Health—
United States. 4. Employee fringe benefits—Law and legislation—
United States. I. Pyenson, Bruce. II. Title.
HD4928.N6W46   1993   93-2892
658.3'25—dc20   CIP

Manufactured in the United States of America

3 4 5 6 7 8 9 10

DEDICATION

to Jack Pyenson

A farmer, small businessman,
and finally, medical
researcher who shares our
skepticism of "experts."

ACKNOWLEDGMENTS

Our heartfelt thanks go to those who took time out from their busy schedules—and, in many cases, billable hours—to provide crucial input on various chapters.

They are: Susan Berger of the Corporation Against Drug Abuse, Bill Dearth of Martin E. Segal & Co., Jon Eisenhandler of Empire Blue Cross/Blue Shield, Susan Linden McGreevy of Husch & Eppenberger, Roy Goldman of Prudential Insurance Co., Sanford Herman of Guardian Life Insurance Co., Joel Isaacson of Clarfeld & Co. (who is awarded the coveted Purple Heart of Crucial Input), James Klein of the Association of Private Pension and Welfare Plans, Bryan Lane of TPF&C, Lawrence E. Kraus and Donna Cuiffo of Clarfeld & Co., Mike Langan of TPF&C, Madeline Lo Re of Patgo Insurance Agency, Steven I. Feiertag of Feiertag Financial Services, Janet Goldberg of Sachnoff and Weaver, Craig Miller of Westminster U.S.A. Ltd., Arthur Moll of Arthur I. Moll Inc., Ken Ronan of The Ronan Agency Inc., Fred Rumack of Buck Consultants, John Satagaj of the Small Business Legislative Council, Linda Sullivan of TPF&C, Suanne Tiberio Trimmer of Clark, Klein & Beaumont, and Marcia Venturi of Buck Consultants.

CONTENTS

PREFACE

Employee benefits have a long and cherished history in the United States. Profit-sharing, pension, and health benefit plans can be traced back a century or more. But the practice didn't really take off within corporate America until World War II, when labor was in short supply, wages were frozen, and management needed a carrot to lure good workers into the factories.

During the 1940s, labor unions won the right to bargain collectively on benefits, so these perks became an intrinsic part of the blue-collar wage package and not an optional frill. It wasn't long before non-union salaried workers were enjoying the same company largesse as their hourly-wage counterparts and benefiting not only from protection from big hospital bills, but from extras like full coverage for visits to chiropractors, podiatrists, and optometrists as well.

Benefit costs in the United States pretty much rose in lockstep with the climb in the Consumer Price Index until the 1970s, when they started going bananas—thanks to the combined influence of federal entitlement programs like Medicare and Medicaid, the growth in the elderly population, and the development of new technologies such as organ transplants. As a result, business health spending grew more than eight-fold between 1970 and 1987—doubling between 1980 and 1987 alone to $134.6 billion.

Today, instead of adding benefits to maintain a competitive edge in the marketplace, companies are frantically attempting to put a lid on benefit costs, which threaten to price their products out of the market.

For many small businesses, the issue isn't even containing health-care coverage but affording it in the first place, since insurance premiums for small groups are often between 10% and 40% higher per capita than those of large firms. It's not surprising that the National Federation of Independent Businesses has ranked health insurance costs as the number one small-business concern.

Can *Employee Benefits for Small Business* offer the magic words that will command the health-cost genie to go back into the bottle? Not quite. But we can give tips to small business owners on how to save money by shopping around for the best value. We'll tell you how to set up a flexible benefit plan: a cost-effective scheme that's also a tax break your employees couldn't get on their own. We'll demonstrate how adopting a wellness program can help small companies like yours stay more productive—because all it may take is a simple blood pressure screening test to convince one of your stroke-prone employees to take action that will keep him or her on the job.

Sometimes playing the benefits game simply means staying on top of the rules. To that end, we've dedicated a chapter to federal and state legislative initiatives affecting your costs down the road, such as the move to make health insurance compulsory. Let's face it, what happens to health benefits in the future depends a great deal on whose voices are heard loudest in Washington and in your state capitol.

Health care coverage isn't the only area where "business as usual" no longer applies. Congress has revised pension laws to make sure management doesn't give "preferential treatment" to their key employees or to themselves—and, of course, to ensure that Congress has access to more taxes. We offer you low-cost pension plan solutions that will keep Uncle Sam off your back and help keep your employees happy at the same time: e.g., SEPs, SARSEPs, 401(k)s, and profit sharing plans.

The definition of "disability" changed in 1990 as well, with the enactment of the Americans With Disabilities Act. As a result, a job applicant with a handicap must be considered along with his or her able-bodied counterpart. We'll tell you how to comply with the law, which protects the rights of disabled people in the workplace, including those infected with AIDS.

Keeping drugs out of the workplace is no longer merely an option for many small companies. If you don't make an effort you could lose a major customer: Uncle Sam. A federal law, the 1988 Drug Free Workplace Act, states that a company doing more than $25,000 worth of business with the government has to have a drug-free workplace program in place. We'll tell you how to get one started and refer you to professionals who can provide more assistance.

In summary, our aim in *Employee Benefits for Small Business* is to explain employee benefits and the laws affecting them in plain English, separating valuable plans from money-wasters, custom-tailoring the advice to suit the size of your company, and featuring hands-on advice from other successful entrepreneurs whenever possible.

Our aim is not to teach you how to be an insurance expert but to help free you to spend less time worrying about employee benefits and more of it doing the job you know best—working to make your business a success.

INTRODUCTION: WHY MEDICAL COVERAGE COSTS SO MUCH

While this book aims to help small businesses purchase a variety of employeee benefits ranging from life insurance to pensions to disability coverage, it shouldn't surprise you that health benefits occupy a healthy chunk of the book.

Health care is the most rapidly growing component of employee compensation in the United States. Spending nearly tripled between 1980 and 1990 alone—from $73 billion to $209.3 billion. In 1990, employee health care costs paid by U.S. corporations were the equivalent of more than 106.2% of total after-tax corporate profits.

In this introduction we'll take a stab at explaining how health benefits became a major cost monster for companies—and a virtual impossibility for many small companies. We'll also present some solutions to America's health care crisis, because the world's best advice to a company about cutting costs won't solve the problem until we as a nation can control them better.

America's health care costs have skyrocketed because we have surrendered control over the demand for medical care—and its price—to our doctors, hospitals, and other health care suppliers. We have handed providers blank checks written largely on two bank accounts: that of employers and that of the federal government. Many economists believe that the federal Medicare program introduced in the early 1960s ignited today's health care inflation by funding the "growth" industry that produces medical care for the elderly.

Two other developments have played a major role in fueling the health cost spiral. First, the development of a plethora of expensive procedures, medical devices, drug therapies, and tests have fed the view of many "consumers" of health care that high-cost medicine always means high quality. Second, the requirement by many state legislatures (responding to special-interest lobbies) that insurers include certain benefits in their coverage had the effect of making coverage increasingly unaffordable to small businesses.

When it comes to new technology, nobody argues against its application if it cures diseases more efficiently than what it replaced. But if it doesn't, what we're witnessing is the economic anomaly of supply creating demand, or the medical establishment charging more money for the same result.

Dr. Arnold Relman, an authority on health care costs and editor of the prestigious *New England Journal of Medicine,* says, "We have a system now that enables companies to build something, push it, get it into use, and collect from third-party insurers for years before there are any controlled tests of whether it's effective."

Relman also blames members of his profession for cashing in on this self-perpetuating technology machine. "There is a growing practice of doctors investing in . . . facilities that provide CAT scans and magnetic-resonance imaging and nuclear tests of one sort or another. Doctors, as part owners of these facilities, profit by referring their patients to them." Kelman wants doctors to stick to practicing medicine: "I'm amazed that the medical community is so slow to agree."

Another culprit driving health care costs sky-high is the requirement by various state legislatures that insurers provide mental health and substance abuse coverage, among other benefits, commonly known as "mandated benefits." In many cases this practice gives carte blanche to those professionals and institutions that provide this coverage.

Employer costs for mental health and substance abuse treatment increased twice as fast as the medical component of the Consumer Price Index during the 1980s, thanks in large part to the 29 states that now mandate coverage for mental health benefits, the 17 states that require it for drug abuse and the 39 states that do so for alcoholism (some of these overlap). These laws produced a bonanza for mental health practitioners; their numbers increased by a whopping 500% in five short years, from 50,000 in 1982 to 250,000 in 1987. Employer costs for mental health and substance abuse treatment are increasing more rapidly than for any other segment of health care, constituting anywhere from 8–40% of employer health bills.

It's not that the insurance industry and members of Congress haven't tried to take a stab at containing costs. Congress enacted maximum ceilings on Medicare payments for certain treatments in 1983. At the same time, insurance companies started requiring covered individuals to get their approval before being admitted to a hospital, to undergo outpatient surgery for minor procedures instead of staying overnight in a hospital, and to seek a second medical opinion for non-emergency surgery.

Unfortunately, when you try to push health costs down in one area, health care providers frequently compensate by raising them somewhere else—and they did just that during the 1980s. When insurance companies tried to cut back on inpatient stays, hospitals made up for it by expanding outpatient centers and raising their prices. Instead of telling patients to "take two aspirins and call in the morning," doctors told people to make an office visit instead: Doctor visits in the U.S. climbed 26% and costs per visit soared 88% between 1981 and 1987, reports The Blue Cross and Blue Shield Association.

Today, small businesses can avoid getting caught in the health cost spiral simply by not buying coverage for their employees—and keeping their fingers crossed. That option might not be available in the future, however. As a way of providing coverage for the 30 million or more Americans who are uninsured, Senator Edward Kennedy (D-Mass.) and Rep. Henry Waxman (D-Calif.) have authored legislation that would require virtually every company to purchase health coverage.

While we certainly sympathize with the plight of the nation's uninsured, we think the enormity of the problem could well be exaggerated by those in politics who are offering a political solution in search of a constituency. For one thing, it's not fair to blame small business for the fact that 15% of Americans under the age of 65 don't have health insurance. Of the uninsured working population—8.2 million people—less than half, 3.9 million people, work for companies with fewer than 25 employees. Thus, fewer than half of the working uninsured work for small business.

What's more, of the 40% of the uninsured who work for firms with more than 100 workers, a big chunk of these are new hires at companies whose practice is to make new employees wait several months before they can get coverage.

There's also a significant portion of the working uninsured population who *choose* this status instead of having it imposed upon them: young single contract workers, for example, who are essentially "free-lancers" who opt for a bigger paycheck over health coverage.

But perhaps the most direct way to discern if America's small business community is truly leaving its employees out in the cold by not providing coverage is to ask the employers themselves. When the National Federation of Independent Business (NFIB) did just that in 1990, 50% of the small-business survey respondents who didn't have health insurance

Figure I-1

THE WORKING UNINSURED BY FIRM SIZE

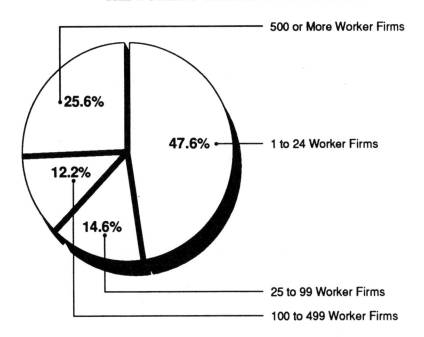

Source: Small Business Administration

Figure I-2

PERCENTAGE OF SMALL BUSINESSES PROVIDING SELECTED EMPLOYEE BENEFITS, 1985

Benefit	Provided to All Employees	Provided to Some Employees	Not Provided
Paid Vacations	59%	18%	23%
Health Insurance	42	23	36
Paid Sick Leave	34	14	52
Life Insurance	33	16	52
Employee Discounts	32	7	61
Retirement Plan	18	8	74

Source: National Federation of Independent Business (NFIB), *Small Business Employee Benefits, 1985* (Washington, DC: NFIB, 1985).
Based on a survey of 1,439 firms with 100 or fewer employees.

said they didn't need to offer the benefit because their employees were already covered under a spouse or parent's policy. When asked whether health benefits are a big concern among their employees, 57.5% said they had no inquiries about providing them from employees, 32.7% said they'd only had a few inquiries, and only 7.3% said they had several inquiries.

Despite that fact, most small business owners genuinely want to offer coverage, and their employees wouldn't be able to afford it on their own.

More than half of the survey respondents who didn't offer insurance told the NFIB they would buy coverage voluntarily—if insurance costs were cut in half.

CONTAINING HEALTH CARE COSTS

So how the heck are we going to make health care coverage more affordable?

One effort that's being launched by the nation's state insurance commissioners is to put small companies on a level playing field with larger concerns. Currently, some smaller companies pay a proportionally higher share of the nation's health care bill because insurers reduce their risks by "cherry-picking"—i.e., selecting the healthiest small companies and giving them the best rates and vice versa. Corporate giants, and even medium-sized companies, have a "healthy mix" of healthy and unhealthy employees, so they aren't subject to such a wide variation in rates.

Insurers justify the practice of cherry-picking by pointing out that some small companies decide to buy coverage only when they know that one of the employees is sick. At the same time, small companies with healthy employees are less likely to buy the insurance because they don't think they need it. The result: There are too few healthy people to subsidize the unhealthy and rates will go up.

The National Association of Insurance Commissioners (NAIC) has proposed eliminating "abusive rating practices," specifically, low "teaser" rates and excessively high rates for small groups with unhealthy people. The

NAIC would have states limit the range between the lowest and highest rates an insurer can offer, as well as capping rate increases.

The NAIC move is an important step to make health costs more stable for small groups. Unfortunately, it will not make the average costs go down or even necessarily hold cost increases down to a rate that makes health coverage affordable.

We need to perform surgery on America's health care system in order to make coverage accessible, either by changing the way that hospitals and doctors charge for their services or the way that the consumers of health care pay for them. What follows are some of the more interesting proposals proffered by health care experts on how we can finally cure what ails America's health care system, followed by our own two cents. In general, these proposals fall into one of two ideological camps: the liberals, who want taxpayers to foot the bill through a government-run system, and the conservatives, who would give tax breaks to taxpayers so that they foot the bill directly.

Heritage Foundation

The Heritage Foundation, the architect of Reaganomics, calls for:

- Eliminating the present tax exclusion for employer-provided health insurance and requiring employers to give their workers the money the companies now spend on insurance for them. In other words, if the company spends $2,000 per worker on insurance premiums, the worker receives that amount to spend on his own.

- Just so that worker doesn't fritter away the $2,000, there would be a federal law requiring everybody to own health insurance, similar to the way car owners have to buy auto insurance. At the same time, all Americans would get a 20% tax credit for health insurance premiums and 30% for out-of pocket medical expenses.

The upshot: If Americans spend their own money on health care, the theory goes, they'll bargain-hunt. They'll be rewarded with more money in their pockets if they are prudent consumers. At the same time, doctors and others who produce competitive products would be rewarded with more patients.

Alain Enthoven

Alain C. Enthoven, professor of public and private management at Stanford University, who advised former British Prime Minister Margaret Thatcher on reforming the British health system, says we should:

- Limit the health coverage premiums for which companies receive tax benefits to 80% of the average cost to provide coverage in a given geographic area. That way employers will spend less and employees will spend more.

- Create mandatory employer coverage, paid for with a fund that also subsidizes insurance for the unemployed, through an employee and employer contribution of 8% of payroll.

- Force all federal and state funded programs such as Medicare and Medicaid to control costs by using managed-care schemes such as HMOs.

Arnold Relman

Dr. Arnold Relman, the editor of the *New England Journal of Medicine,* says we should:

- Create a national think tank that generates information about new health technology—and whether it's worth paying for—and feed it to insurers. "Unless we make a major investment in the new trials of the safety, cost and relative effectiveness of the drugs, tests and procedures we now employ so generously . . . we will never know enough to make discriminating choices."
- If a technique or technology is worthless, insurers shouldn't have to pay for its use. The $500 million to support the think tank, which could come either from the government or the insurance industry, "would pay for itself many times over."
- All employers should use HMOs and should make their employees pay out of their own pockets if they want to use a non-HMO doctor.

The Canadian System

Several recent polls have shown that most Americans like the idea of Canadian-style national health insurance, an idea that doubtless received more credibility when business leaders like Lee Iacocca came out for it. In Canada 74% of health costs are paid by the federal and provincial governments and the system still consumes only 9% of its gross national product, as opposed to the U.S., where 42% of health care is paid for by the government and it consumes 11% of GNP.

Does Canada get more by spending less? No, says an editorial in Canada's *Maclean's* magazine: "Hospitals across the country are taking beds out of service, limiting the number of operations they perform and cutting back on other services as governments battle to keep down health care costs."

It's so difficult to get costly life-saving treatment in Canada that at least one underground organization has been set up to spirit sick Canadians across the border to get help. Heartbeat Windsor, a private voluntary organization set up in Windsor, Ontario, has helped more than 400 waitlisted Canadians obtain critically needed surgery in the U.S.

Even if health care Canada-style could be grafted onto the U.S. delivery system, it's questionable if Americans would want to foot the bill. A Canadian-model distribution of costs would saddle the states with responsibility for the entire $250 billion in new spending, since the U.S. and Canadian federal governments pay roughly 29% of the national health care bill. That translates into a 71% increase in state tax revenues.

HEALTH CARE REFORM IN THE 1990S

As we were preparing this new edition, President Bill Clinton was promising to reform America's health care system, but he hadn't yet spelled out the specifics. What follows are some of the leading trial balloons offered by Clinton's advisors and our assessment of their effectiveness:

Managed competition: Under managed competition, the government, in effect, limits the number of insurers or HMOs in a certain market so that each of them has enough market share to negotiate lower fees with doctors and hospitals. Called "Organized Systems of Care," these insurers or HMOs would each offer comparable benefit packages.

Our view: While managed competition may give large insurers enough clout to make deals with doctors, it may well shut out the entrepreneurs who offer better service, better technology, or lower costs than traditional health care providers or insurers.

Community rating: Under some versions of this policy, insurers cannot vary their rates according to an individual's age, sex, industry, health status, or health habits but instead must base them on the average per-person medical bill of a large group of people—such as a collection of small groups.

Our view: While the use of community rating may eliminate some of the abuses of the past—such as a whopping rate increase when one member of a group becomes seriously ill—the end result may be that companies with a preponderance of young, healthy employees will pay more to subsidize those with older workers.

Spending caps: A national board determines the dollar amount that the government and private sectors can spend on health care. In theory, spending caps would be enforced by a combination of price controls — for example, the fee that a doctor can charge for a given procedure—and budget limits on both government and private-sector spending.

Our view: One danger of this approach is that special-interest groups in the health care business—whether hospitals, drug companies, medical associations, or wheel-chair manufacturers—would each lobby to receive the most generous portion of the budgetary spoils. Whoever had the most effective lobby would win. Even if price and cost controls were workable, the budgeting process and the pool of health care dollars would still be controlled by the folks who are driving up health costs in the first place.

Tax on benefits: Under this scenario, companies would no longer be able to deduct the full cost of overly generous benefits from their taxes. Currently, the employer's costs of providing health benefits are entirely tax-deductible to the employer and are not considered taxable income to the employee. The theory of the proposed tax is that, aside from bringing in cash for the government, such a tax would discourage overly generous and hence inflationary benefits.

Our view: Pardon our skepticism, but this seems more like a tax and less like a cure for our health woes.

Mandatory coverage: All employers would be required to buy employee health care coverage, under the theory that the average cost of insurance will go down because the pool of premium-payers would now include those business owners with mostly healthy employees who don't bother to buy insurance. Clinton's health care reform advisers insist that mandatory coverage won't be implemented until other measures have mitigated the affordability problem.

Our view: Making health care coverage slightly less expensive is a small consolation to cash-strapped small businesses who can't afford to buy the coverage in the first place—even with government subsidies to small businesses.

Whether these proposals would help or hurt our health care system, we believe that they won't be implemented anytime soon because of the political clout of the special-interest groups in the medical and insurance community. The politically safest course of action for Clinton will be to make the current system more fair. Here are some workable, likely reforms:

1. Make insurance more accessible by restricting the ability of insurers to reject sick individuals—except those individuals who wait until they are sick to try to buy insurance.

2. Reduce costs by encouraging small businesses to join together in purchasing coalitions so they can benefit from some of the cost advantages enjoyed by larger companies. For one thing, these coalitions would be exempt from certain regulations that increase costs for small businesses such as state laws that require the purchase of particular benefits. (Purchasing coalitions are described more fully in Chapter Four.)

3. Reduce the number of uninsured Americans by increasing the income limits of individuals who may be entitled to Medicaid coverage.

4. Control government costs by encouraging more Medicaid and Medicare recipients to enroll in Health Maintenance Organizations.

5. Reduce costs by not allowing doctors to own testing labs from which they profit when they refer patients for tests.

Our Two Cents

There is a lot of room for improvement in America's health care system: unnecessary and overpriced health care chews up an estimated 20 percent or more of our health care expenditures. Unfortunately, the incremental reforms that probably will be carried out over the next few years won't take a scalpel to the high price of medical care.

On the other hand, we don't prescribe a socialized medicine antidote to America's feverish health costs; we don't advocate having government bureaucrats trying to micro-manage what is now still a free-enterprise system.

For one thing, we spent a year observing England's 40-year "experiment" in socialized medicine where one of us worked in the health insurance field. By U.S. standards, the medical care provided by Britain's National Health Service is low-cost—but at what cost? Citizens face long queues for threadbare, low-tech health care: there are no trauma care centers, and modern, same-day surgery is just beginning to be introduced.

At the same time some reformers in the United States are looking to European, state-controlled solutions to iron out the glitches in our medical care system, these same state-controlled systems are considering adding a healthy dose of U.S.-style free enterprise to their methodology.

As with other European nations who are grappling with the problems of runaway prices and the poor quality of state-run care, the British have been decentralizing and de-bureaucratizing their health care system. Managers in the NHS have been flocking to U.S. health care providers to learn modern techniques—and hiring U.S. consultants to implement them.

Why? An increasing number of hospitals, doctors, HMOs, and insurers are learning the secrets that the Japanese "taught" U.S. manufacturers in the 1980s: that achieving quality and cost efficiency aren't two unrelated goals, but two sides of the same coin. The treatment of a given medical condition in the most efficient way possible—for example, releasing patients from the hospital as quickly as possible so they won't be exposed to further illness—also happens to be good medicine.

We'd like to see hospitals and doctors adopt standardized protocols of medical treatment that specify how to treat uncomplicated cases so there isn't a lot of variation in how to treat the same ailment. If these policies were applied across the board, we'd go a long way toward taking the art out of practicing medicine and treating medicine more like a science, creating uniform definitions of the best treatments for diseases.

Would members of America's medical establishment stand for such uniformity? They will if they're smart. Such protocols could be the basis for "safe harbor" protection from malpractice suits for physicians—the very phenomenon that doctors blame for the high cost of delivering medical care.

We also believe that the public and employers deserve to receive reports about the quality of individual hospitals and physicians—their cure rates and mortality rates. This way employers and employees alike can better tell which hospitals competently cure sick people without charging them an arm and a leg for it.

While government bureaucrats will, no doubt, continue to twiddle the dials on the techniques used to market health insurance, the people who are most effectively stanching the wasteful flow of health care dollars are those doctors, hospitals, insurers, and HMOs in the private sector who compete by doing a better job manufacturing their "product." No government-imposed "market reform" is going to teach productivity.

The quality/efficiency litmus test must be as rigorously applied to the business of delivering medical care as it has been to the manufacture of automobiles, computers, and other consumer products. We'd suggest that small business owners—who understand that their survival depends on providing quality service at a competitive price—could teach the health care industry a thing or two. We hope it happens soon.

CHAPTER 1
AN EXECUTIVE SUMMARY OF MEDICAL COVERAGE

WHY BUY HEALTH COVERAGE?

In a very real sense, the decision to offer employee benefits represents a watershed for many small companies. Let's face it, while many people who start their own companies buy health coverage for themselves, they don't initially extend it to other employees because of the tremendous financial expense involved.

At the same time, the entrepreneur knows that to attract and retain top-flight employees it's necessary to do better than convince employees that it's exciting to be involved in a startup. Good employees—especially those with families or intentions to start one—are likely to leave a small company for the job and benefits security of a larger firm unless there are perks that make it worthwhile to stay.

Here are the reasons why most companies provide health benefits:

- To recruit employees.
- To improve morale and satisfaction.
- To ease employees' fears about the high cost of health care.
- To make sure employees stay healthy and productive.
- It's tax effective: group medical benefits substitute pre-tax dollars for after-tax costs.

Once you've decided to buy coverage, the next chore is to figure out what kinds of benefits you want. What follows is a thumbnail sketch of the different ways to buy coverage. We will explain these in more depth in separate chapters, as well as the options for containing costs using each approach.

The Basics of Coverage

Medical coverage should be designed to cover, as a minimum, the catastrophic costs of care for a serious acute illness or accident. Basic medical coverages pay for at least some portion of the following services:

- Hospital room and board
- Hospital outpatient care
- Surgeon's and anesthetist's fees
- Operating room fees, inpatient drugs, and dressings
- Physician office visits for non-routine exams
- Physician hospital visits
- Emergency room treatment

• Diagnostic lab and X-ray—inpatient and outpatient

Other benefits that can be offered are:

• Outpatient prescriptions
• Maternity
• Well-baby care
• Home health care/ extended care facility
• Mental health
• Private duty nursing
• Dental
• Vision

There are also other health benefits which fall under the category of "wellness." These are usually not part of the insurance coverage:

• Screening for colon cancer, breast cancer, high blood pressure, high blood cholesterol
• Training in first aid such as cardiopulmonary resuscitation
• Safety (proper lifting techniques to avoid workplace injury, seatbelt use)
• Lifestyle (smoking cessation, weight loss)

Your Priorities

There are a variety of ways to purchase benefits. The delivery system you choose will depend on how important the following issues are to you: permitting your employees freedom to choose their own doctors and hospitals, freeing yourself from the headaches of administering the plan, and containing your costs.

Or, to put it another way, the priorities are:

1. Employee freedom to choose or stay with his current doctor or hospital.
2. Employee cash flow: Does the employee have to pay the doctor or hospital and wait for reimbursement from the insurer?
3. Employee paperwork and complexity: Are claim forms, deductibles, coinsurance a problem for employees?
4. Importance of preventative medicine and comprehensive coverage.
5. Quality of coverage: Do you have to provide the best coverage, or is a bare-bones program sufficient?
6. Headache-free administration for you.

TRADITIONAL VERSUS ALTERNATIVE DELIVERY SYSTEMS

There are two main styles of benefits you can buy (with hundreds of variations and hybrids). There are *traditional plans* which include service benefits and indemnity benefits, and there are *alternative delivery systems* which include systems known as Health Maintenance Organizations (HMOs) and Preferred Provider Organizations (PPOs). To make matters more complicated, many insurance companies and Blue Cross/Blue Shield organizations (the Blues) offer both traditional plans and PPO and HMO programs.

Here's a quick summary of the appeal of each. We ask you to remember that there are a lot of exceptions to these generalizations. Also, smaller companies have fewer options than larger companies. The details of each of the alternatives are in the chapters that follow.

The Traditional Plans

The traditional approach is for an insurer to pay for services rendered by any qualified doctor or hospital. There are two basic kinds:

Traditional service benefits (usually offered by the Blues) used to differ from commercial plans because the benefits were narrower. Now the major difference between the two is that you usually don't have to fill out paperwork because physicians and hospitals in many states typically bill the Blues directly.

Service benefits are for employers who want little paperwork and employees who want their own choice in doctors, hospitals, and treatment. You usually don't have to pay the bills and send in forms for reimbursement if the insurer has participating provider networks among doctors and hospitals.

Indemnity benefits, usually including comprehensive major medical plans, mean the insurer reimburses the insured for bills. They often involve a deductible and coinsurance (an out-of-pocket payment on the part of the employee) and will only pay up to a certain amount for a given procedure. The insured has to pay any shortfall. Coverage can be complete or bare-bones.

An indemnity plan will usually require an individual to pay the bills first and send in forms for reimbursement from the insurance company. These plans are for people who don't mind some paperwork, but want freedom to choose their own hospital or doctor.

Alternative Delivery Systems

Alternative delivery systems involve organizations which both *receive* "insurance" premiums and *provide* medical services. These organizations have made special deals with certain doctors and hospitals. These special deals are supposed to lower costs for the people who are members of the alternative delivery system. There are two kinds:

Health Maintenance Organizations (HMOs) are arrangements between health care providers and customers in which preset fees are paid to the provider for coverage, regardless of the treatment costs. Because there is an incentive to control costs, treatments are scrutinized to make sure they are really necessary.

HMOs are appealing to employees because checkups are often free or inexpensive and they don't have to fill in forms for reimbursement. On the other hand, if they go to a non-HMO doctor there is usually no coverage.

HMOs may be for people who want one-stop shopping and little paperwork but don't mind relatively little choice in doctors, hospitals, and treatment.

Preferred Provider Organizations (PPOs) are also arrangements between a group of providers and their customers, except the agreement is usually for a reduced fee for each service, not a preset fee for all services. Unlike the HMO, if a member goes to a non-PPO doctor, they'll usually get reduced coverage. So the insured can exercise a choice if he or she doesn't mind paying a bit more for that choice.

PPOs are for companies whose employees want more choice of physicians. Paperwork is usually limited, especially for PPO-approved providers. PPOs offer some of the benefits of both indemnity plans and HMOs.

CHOOSING THE BEST STYLE

Each of the above four types can come in low, medium or high-cost versions depending on what they cover. However, by their nature HMOs and to a lesser extent PPOs offer fairly full coverage, so they don't have as much range in cost as do the traditional programs.

There are hundreds of different HMOs, PPOs, and insurance companies selling thousands of different products, and many HMOs and PPOs operate in only small areas. Furthermore, not all of these products are available in all parts of the country. Finally, there are good and not-so-good companies of each type. The first thing to decide is which benefits are best for you.

Here is a scorecard to help. Rate the importance of each category:

Maximize Employee Freedom of Choice

1. Importance of choosing your own doctor
2. Importance of choosing your own hospital
3. Importance of out-of-area coverage for dependents (if employees have children in college, for example)

Recommendation: If these categories are very important to you, then an HMO or PPO is probably not the right choice. However, some HMOs or PPOs in your area may include your doctor/hospital plus have good out-of-area coverage. *You'll probably choose an indemnity or service plan.*

Optimize Employee Cash Flow

1. No cash payment to hospital on large bills
2. No cash payment to doctor for most bills
3. No cash payments to pharmacist for small bills

Recommendation: If minimizing even small amounts of employee cash flow is important to you, then you probably want to look at *HMOs, PPOs, or full Blue Cross/Blue Shield coverage.* However, many insurers and hospitals are open to making arrangements in advance to help the insured patient avoid paying large bills and waiting for reimbursement.

Minimize Employee Paperwork

1. No out-of-pocket payments, i.e., deductibles and coinsurance
2. No claim forms

Recommendation: If paperwork will drive you or your employees batty, go for an *HMO, PPO, or Blue Cross/Blue Shield* service plan.

Maximize Employee Coverage and Preventative Care

1. Checkups and routine physicals are covered by plan
2. Preventative medicine approach
3. Comprehensive care

Recommendation: If full coverage and preventative medicine are attractive to you, go for an *HMO.* However, expensive options attached to service or indemnity coverages may pay for routine exams as well.

Minimize Cost to Employer

1. Very low cost is important
2. Full benefits are not important

Recommendation: By far the cheapest plans are the *high deductible indemnity plans.*

Minimize Employer Paperwork, Administration

1. Few hassles with insurer over claims payments
2. Few hassles with insurer over premium payments
3. One-stop shopping for life insurance, disability, etc.

Unfortunately, we can't make a blanket recommendation because among both commercial plans and the Blues there have been administrative disasters. Recommendation: *Go by reputation.* Ask other small businessmen whether their carrier has been good.

In the next chapter we'll go into much more detail on each of these choices.

CHAPTER 2
THE RIGHT MEDICAL COVERAGE FOR YOUR BUSINESS

In Chapter 1 we summarized the strengths and weaknesses of the major benefits. In this chapter we go into much more detail about these benefits so that you can have an idea about which benefit plan you want before you select an agent and an insurer.

The traditional products are the fee-for-service products, in which the medical provider (doctor, hospital, pharmacist, dentist, optician, etc.) performs a service and charges a fee, some or all of which may be covered by insurance. This approach contrasts with alternative delivery systems such as HMOs and PPOs, in which the insurer or other organization contracts ahead of time with a select group of doctors or hospitals and other providers for specified services.

THE TRADITIONAL PRODUCTS

There are two major kinds of traditional products: service benefits and major medical benefits. The service benefits, the traditional mainstay of the Blue Cross and Blue Shield Associations—or the Blues—pay full hospital expenses up to certain limits and pay fully for certain kinds of physician fees. Major medical benefits, on the other hand, usually cover a wide range of hospital, physician, and related expenses but require a contribution by the patient, better known as deductibles and coinsurance.

The most common carriers of medical benefits are the Blue Cross/Blue Shield plans and the commercial insurers.

The Blues

Strengths:

- If you're a "high-risk" company (explained later), the Blues will probably insure you, whereas a commercial carrier might not
- Your Blues card is accepted by hospitals in most areas
- A wide range of benefits is offered
- Doctors and hospitals often bill the Blues plan directly, relieving your employees of paperwork hassles

Weaknesses:

- Sometimes they have poor administration and poor service
- In some states they cannot sell non-medical insurance such as life or disability

- Small companies that are considered good medical risks might get a better rate from commercial carriers.
- May not offer group benefits to very small companies—for example, those with fewer than 5 employees

Before the 1970s Blue Cross and Blue Shield were separate organizations covering hospital services and medical/ surgical services. Today, combined Blue Cross/Blue Shield organizations operate in most states, although some states have two or more Blues organizations that compete against one another.

The various state laws that established the Blues often helped create provider networks of doctors and hospitals for the Blues, which usually included most of the doctors and hospitals in a state. Most Blues plans pay participating providers directly, rather than reimbursing the patient for charges that the patient already paid, a feature that has traditionally appealed to companies who don't want to hassle their employees with paperwork.

The Blues have traditionally enjoyed a competitive price advantage because so-called participating physicians and hospitals agreed to accept a discounted fee. Other cost advantages stem from the fact that in most states the Blues pay little or no agent commissions, but rather sell directly to businesses, and they are exempt from paying state premium taxes.

Recently, however, the Blues' price advantage has been eroding. In exchange for the state-backed price advantages, the Blues were often required to act as an insurer of last resort and to accept risks that commercial insurance companies wouldn't. Recently, more and more commercial carriers are succeeding in attracting the Blues' best risks, and the Blues are left with an increasing share of the worst groups and individuals.

In recent years the Blues have struggled to compete with commercial carriers by offering alternative delivery systems such as HMOs and PPOs and a full range of benefits, including dental, vision, and prescription programs. They also have instituted cost sharing features such as deductibles and coinsurance through major medical policies.

But in the battle against commercial insurers, Blue Cross has steadily lost market share, dropping from 50% in 1970 to 36% in 1988. As their market share dwindled, Blue Cross plans have seen their financial shape deteriorate.

In the fall of 1990 Blue Cross of West Virginia went into receivership, leaving $50 million in medical bills unpaid. More than 15 other plans are on the watch list of the Blue Cross and Blue Shield Association, the Chicago-based organization that licenses and oversees these plans. Despite these problems, most Blues plans are carefully watched by state regulators. Your best bet is to research your local plan thoroughly and talk to other businesses who have had experience with them.

Commercial Carriers

Advantages:

- Efficient administration and service in many cases.

- Competitive rates, particularly if you have mostly healthy employees
- One-stop shopping for a wide range of benefits: disability, life insurance, investments
- You have an intermediary in the form of your local agent/broker

Disadvantages:

- You may pay more due to agent commissions and other factors
- Your company or some of its employees may be rejected if your company's line of business is too risky or your employees aren't healthy
- Some commercial carriers' rates can be very volatile

Commercial companies in the health insurance business are usually life insurers, though there are property and casualty companies (i.e., the guys who sell car and homeowner's insurance) in the business as well.

Many commercial insurers have sought to set up or buy HMOs and PPOs (explained in the next section) in recent years. But the mainstay of commercial insurers has been the comprehensive major medical benefits that cover many services and include deductibles and coinsurance.

Many insurers will offer full programs for dental, vision, and prescription drug programs. The prescription drug benefit can be offered as either a "stand-alone" program with its own limits or as part of the comprehensive major medical program.

Commercial insurers sell through brokers and independent agents, who sell many companies' products, and through tied agents, who only sell the products of their own company. Agent commissions range from 5% to 10% or more of the annual premium of a group, whether they're independent or tied agents, so commissions are an important part of your expense.

We recommend independent agents or brokers over tied agents for the simple reason that because they represent many companies they have the ability to shop around for the best deal for you—and to find another insurer if you're ultimately unhappy with the one that you have.

Where to get this coverage: What kinds of companies sell traditional health coverage? The Blues and many large insurers. We suggest that you look for an independent agent or broker who specializes in small business. You probably can get life insurance, property insurance and other coverage through such an agent. But note: Some states don't permit the Blues to sell anything but medical insurance and some Blues plans don't work through agents or brokers.

THE NONTRADITIONAL PRODUCTS

HMOs

In an HMO, which generally emphasizes preventative care, a group of doctors and hospitals provides the bulk of the patients' care at a cost that's worked out in advance between the providers and the HMO, unlike traditional service or indemnity plans in which a fee is paid for each service. So HMO doctors are supposed to have an economic incentive to control costs.

The patient must usually select a primary care doctor within the HMO—a gatekeeper—who screens the individual before he or she can see a specialist. There may be an exception for pediatric, gynecological, and obstetric care.

There are nearly 600 HMOs in the U.S., covering 32.5 million people. In 1989, 17% of participants in employer-sponsored health care plans in medium-to-large companies were in HMOs.

While employees may perceive that the lack of freedom to choose their own doctor is a significant drawback, there are advantages to HMOs over commercial carriers that can outweigh the disadvantages. Here's what employees get for giving up the freedom to choose their own doctors:

- Low out-of-pocket expenditures on health care: a flat fee as low as $2 per office visit—or nothing, perhaps capped at $500 or so a year. Given the high cost of medical care, this is an increasingly attractive feature of HMOs to employees.
- Preventative care coverage. Many traditional plans don't pay for routine treatments such as vaccinations.
- No claim forms to file.

Unlike the traditional insurance benefits provided by commercial insurers and the Blues, HMOs both finance and provide services; they contract with the doctors and nurses to deliver the services and contract with one or more hospitals to provide hospital care, although a few HMOs own and operate their own hospitals. On the other hand, conventional insurance plans simply reimburse health care providers.

HMOs generally provide more comprehensive services than do commercial insurance plans or Blue Cross/Blue Shield plans. A federal law, The HMO Act of 1973, specifies what kind of coverage has to be offered in "federally qualified" HMOs. For example, they must provide routine exams, emergency care, short-term outpatient mental health care, medical treatment and referral for alcohol and drug abuse and addiction, diagnostic laboratory services, and home health care. HMOs can also provide vision care, dental care, physical therapy, and prescription drugs.

There are three kinds of HMOs:

Individual Practice Associations, or IPAs. The biggest component of the HMO group, these are groups of physicians working out of their own offices who provide services to HMO subscribers but also provide services to patients who aren't HMO subscribers. The physicians may work for several different HMOs. These are often referred to as open-panel plans, because subscribers can choose any IPA doctor.

Although these physicians don't operate from a central facility, the HMO is still supposed to oversee the appropriateness and quality of care and the use of services. The IPA physician may share in the financial gain or loss when the cost of providing covered health services to HMO subscribers is less or greater than the fees budgeted by the HMO.

Group model HMOs. These contract with physician groups—professional corporations with a large number of doctors—to provide services to HMO subscribers. The HMO usually reimburses the physicians at a fixed rate per patient. The physicians may split their time between HMO subscribers and non-subscribers. Physicians may also work for more than one HMO.

Staff model HMOs. Under this arrangement, the HMO hires the physicians rather than contracting with them, so these doctors are fulltime employees of the HMO and they usually operate out of centralized facilities. The staff model HMOs have the most control over how their doctors practice medicine. In theory, the greatest cost savings should be with these HMOs. Group and staff model plans are also known as closed-panel plans.

Because HMOs are geared to provide comprehensive service, they find it hard to offer a "budget plan" that could compete with low-cost and low-coverage traditional plans that require an out-of-pocket payment from the covered employee. An example of a low-cost and low-coverage plan is a comprehensive major medical plan with 80% coinsurance and a $1,000 deductible.

What some HMOs do to lower costs is to require copayments, a small fee on the part of the patient, for each physician visit. This practice also tends to lower the frequency of visits, since the exams are no longer free. HMOs can offer less expensive programs by increasing the copayments and by excluding prescription drugs, vision, and other benefits.

Advantages of HMOs to employees:

- HMOs offer one-stop health-care-service shopping to participants
- Broader benefits than with a conventional plan
- Few deductibles
- Preventative medical care
- Little or no paperwork.

Disadvantages to employees:

- Little freedom to choose physicians and hospitals
- Possibly limited or no out-of-area coverage.

Advantages to employers:

- Possibly lower cost
- Broader coverage
- Less administrative work for employees

Disadvantages to employers:

- Increased liability: you're more likely to get sued by an employee if you limit his or her choice of physicians and the employee winds up a victim of malpractice.

"Employers' potential liability exposure increases as they limit the choice of physicians, hospitals or treatment," says Marcia Venturi, an actuary with Buck Consultants in Secaucus, New Jersey. Venturi cites a court case in which an employer was found liable in a malpractice lawsuit brought by an employee, despite the fact that the employee had the final say in choosing the doctor and the fact that employers aren't required by law to offer health benefits in the first place.

Are HMOs effective in containing costs? Some insurance experts are skeptical about HMOs' sustained ability to do so, since ultimately HMOs have to offer the same expensive technology as their fee-for-service competitors. Their vaunted lower rate of hospitalization may be due to the fact that younger and healthier people tend to choose them in greater numbers than older people, who tend to have established relationships with doctors. Only one-third of the employers surveyed by the benefits consulting firm Foster Higgins in 1988 said that their HMOs were effective in controlling costs.

How to shop for an HMO: Compare costs and services between HMOs run by the Blues, those run by commercial carriers and those that are independently run. You may have to contact the HMOs directly (the Yellow Pages are a start) if they don't deal through agents.

PPOs

Preferred provider organizations are kind of a hybrid animal, a cross between traditional coverage and an HMO. As with an IPA-model HMO, PPOs contract with health providers for less expensive health care. As with traditional coverage, the billing to the PPO is usually done on a fee-for-service basis and isn't prepaid.

PPOs are a recent and rapidly growing health care option. Most of the 655 PPOs in existence in 1989 have been started since 1983, according to The National Association of Employers on Health Care Action. Results of a 1988 survey by TPF&C, the employee benefits consulting division of New York-based Towers, Perrin, indicate that one-fourth of 163 companies offered their employees a PPO option, while another 22% said they were considering doing so.

Here's how PPOs typically work: Physicians and hospitals agree to charge an insurer or large employer low fees for services in exchange for an increased pool of patients, faster claims processing, or both. Some arrangements are based on a discount off regular charges, on a specific cost per day, or on the cost to treat a specific ailment.

Employees are motivated to use the PPO because of positive or negative financial incentives; typically a doctor visit costs only $5 or $10, as opposed to the full fee for a fee-for-service doctor (could be $65 or more). This doesn't sound like it's saving money for the employer, but similar to an HMO, part of the PPO's operating philosophy is that it's making preventative medicine more attractive to a group of employees who otherwise wouldn't see a doctor if the visits were prohibitively expensive. Other arrangements are less generous: Patients pay 20% of the bill with a PPO doctor and half of the bill if it's a non-PPO doctor.

As with HMOs, the preventative care probably doesn't save money in the short run. PPOs will only work if other cost-containment measures are used besides discounted doctor visit fees, says the Employee Benefit Research Institute. Physicians and hospitals must avoid unnecessary tests and X-rays and emphasize outpatient treatment. PPO sponsors may monitor claims, require prior authorization for certain types of treatment, and examine physician case records.

Not all health care consultants are sold on PPOs, however. While some firms have saved a lot of money with PPOs, the discounts offered by the medical group providing care are typically offset by more frequent office visits, says Jack Mahoney, vice president of Alexander Consulting Group Inc. in Lyndhurst, New Jersey.

Where to find a PPO: Anyone can own a PPO: the Blues, insurers, hospitals, physician groups, investors, third party administrators. Your best bet is to find one through an insurance broker who specializes in small group benefits.

CHAPTER 3
ARE YOU READY TO BUY MEDICAL COVERAGE?

If you've got an idea of what benefits you want, the next step is to figure out how to pay for them. In this chapter, we'll discuss how to find an insurance broker, how rates are set, and how to purchase coverage.

CHOOSING A PLAN

Before you find an insurance broker, ask other small businesses what insurance company or Blues plan they use, rather than relying solely on a broker.

Remember that the health care market is a localized one. The HMO your brother-in-law in Topeka says is the country's best may not operate in your area. Some insurers have regional operations and some national insurers have weak areas and strongholds. Also, some insurers that have set up PPOs have signed up many providers in some areas and hardly any in others.

The basic question to ask other businesses about an insurer or HMO/PPO is "Are you satisfied?" Here are some more pointed questions:

If You're Enrolled in a Commercial or Blues Plan

- Are employees happy with the program?
- Do employees have problems getting reimbursed?
- Were there administrative headaches when the business first signed up with the insurer, such as delays in enrolling employees, sending out membership cards? How were they cleared up?
- How much have rates gone up at the last two or three renewals?
- Have individuals been excluded due to ill health?
- What are the premiums? How often are rates changed?
- How easy is it to get problems resolved?
- Does your broker go to bat for you?
- Are cost-containment measures used such as utilization review? Are they effective?
- Are you required to buy other insurance from the same insurer such as group life coverage?

If You're an HMO or PPO Purchaser

- Are the employees happy with the HMO/PPO? Does the plan conduct satisfaction surveys? What are the results?

- Were there administrative headaches?
- Are the doctors too hurried to spend time with patients?
- How well do the doctors communicate with patients?
- Are the HMO facilities clean?
- Do employees complain about how long it takes to make an appointment?
- Do employees complain about lack of choice in doctors or specialists?
- What do employees like and dislike about the HMO/PPO?
- How much have rates gone up at the last two or three renewals?
- Have individuals been excluded due to ill health?
- What are the premiums?
- How easy is it to get problems resolved?
- Does the agent/broker go to bat for you?

FINDING AN AGENT OR BROKER

The second thing you have to do is find an insurance broker. The best source of information is word of mouth from small business owners. Your broker should also be able to supply you with references: his or her other clients who have bought a particular company's products.

While you might be tempted to buy insurance directly from a company to save money, it doesn't quite work that way.

If you go directly to the insurer's home office you'll most likely be referred straight to an agent. Most insurers don't want to compete with the people who bring them business. This arrangement can work in your favor. Independent agents have more clout with the insurer or HMO because they will take business elsewhere if they're not happy. So one of the major ways insurers keep independents happy is by keeping their clients happy.

For that reason, we recommend that you use an independent agent or broker rather than one who represents only one company. They should be listed as independents in the phone book.

There are some insurers, however, who have traditionally not used agents very much—the Blues, for example—and sometimes directly contact small businesses by phone. There might be a small incentive payment to the telephone solicitor, but this is much less than an insurance commission.

However, even if an insurer such as the Blues doesn't work through agents, this doesn't necessarily mean you'll save money. This is because agents tend to save the insurance company money by screening out bad risks, savings that are reflected in premiums.

The Request for a Proposal

After you've talked to other small businesses and discussed with your agent what benefits you want, ask for a comparison of rates and services from the companies you've chosen as well as others that the agent recommends. If you're considering an HMO or PPO, this is the time to get lists of participating doctors and hospitals from local PPOs and HMOs.

As we discuss at greater length in Chapter Four, make sure your request for a proposal contains a list of benefits that you *don't* want as well as services and cost-saving measures that you do want. For example, if none of your employees wear glasses or contact lenses, it probably doesn't make sense to buy vision coverage. Make sure you ask for a company with service features such as toll-free "800" helplines for employee questions about coverage.

At the same time, if you're opting for more generous benefits, expect to pay for them.

"Plans that pay hospital expenses in full or that have low deductibles are very expensive," says Fred Rumack, director of tax and legal services for Buck Consultants Inc. of Manhattan.

Small businesses are usually offered a limited set of benefits and options, so you won't be able to demand a custom-tailored package of benefits. However, sellers have tried to make these packages attractive to small businesses, so you should be able to find the benefits you want.

If the price from the insurer comes back too high, ask to see quotes from other companies or ask for cost-cutting measures such as higher deductibles or coinsurance payments, which we discuss at greater length in Chapter Four.

Your Agent Sizes You Up

Once you have found an agent, you shouldn't have to worry about the conversation falling flat. He'll want to know how many employees you have, their age and sex, how long your company has been in business, what kind of business it is, etc. A typical application for coverage is reproduced in Figure 3-1.

Why so nosy? The agent is trying to figure out how risky your business is—both from the standpoint of the viability of the business itself and the health of the employees. Note: Not all companies have the same criteria for "underwriting"—an insurance term that means assessing risk. So if you've been turned down for coverage don't jump to the conclusion that you can't get insurance unless you've shopped around. What's more, the Blues may insure you if a conventional carrier won't.

Here's a list of some of the risks insurers consider:

New business risk: If your company is very new or in shaky financial shape, it may go out of business. The time, effort, and expense that the insurer and broker/agent put into selling and starting up your coverage will be wasted if you go out of business or can't pay the premium bills after a few months. Many carriers won't provide coverage for groups that have been in business for less than a year, since 80% of new businesses fail in the first three years.

Type of industry risk: There are a surprising number of occupations that are considered risky by insurance carriers, either because there's a high turnover of employees or the people work with toxic substances or in environments that are dangerous or prone to disease. Companies in high risk categories may either be denied coverage or pay more for it.

Here is a sampling of some of the workplaces and occupations deemed risky by a leading health insurer.

Adult bookstores
Movie theaters
Amusement parks and
  concessions
Pool parlors
Embassies and consulates
Self-employed nurses and doctors
Mines
Race tracks
Garbage collectors
Taxicab companies

Mental health, alcohol, and drug
  abuse centers
Athletic teams
Barber shops
Electroplating firms
Fabricated wire and metal
  production
Hypnosis clinics
Oil and gas drilling companies
Real estate companies, agents
  and appraisers
Sports promoters

In addition, if you're a farmer or run a non-profit group, a bowling alley, a labor union, a used car dealership, a hotel, a restaurant, or a nursing home you may have a tough time getting coverage, primarily because these are seasonal, unstable businesses or have lots of part-time employees.

Medical cost risk: These categories include age/sex/marital status, the health status of employees, and previous medical costs. Older people have higher medical expenses, women usually cost more to insure than men at certain ages, and married women have higher maternity costs than single women, so the age, sex, and marital status of your employees has a lot to do with what rates you'll pay.

Your employees may be asked to fill out a "short form" medical questionnaire, which includes data on the applicant's age, weight, height, illnesses or injuries that required medical treatment, and whether or not the individual or close relatives have had certain diseases: high blood pressure, heart disease, diabetes, lung ailments, cancer, etc.

One major insurer of small groups asks on its application whether or not any of the covered employees—or dependents, if applicable—have had ulcers, arthritis, a Caesarean section, AIDS, or cancer, among other ailments or procedures. The questionnaire also asks about alcoholic beverage use exceeding 14 drinks a week or whether the individual has smoked cigarettes within the past 12 months or gained or lost more than 15 pounds within the last 12 months.

Figure 3-1

Golden Rule®

PARTICIPATING EMPLOYER APPLICATION

Golden Rule Insurance Company
Home Office
Golden Rule Building
Lawrenceville, Illinois 62439

Trustee: Merchants National Bank & Trust Co., Indianapolis, Indiana

Section 1   EMPLOYER INFORMATION

Company's legal name _____

Business Address _____

       Street   City   State   Zip   County

Mailing Address _____

       Street   City   State   Zip   County

Contact Person _____

Phone ( ) _____

Nature of Business _____

How Long in Business_____   (Give Details)

Present Group Insurance Carrier (if none, so indicate) _____

_____

Present Coverage Termination Date_____ / _____ / _____

Which best describe why coverage is being terminated?

_____ Rate Increase   _____ Poor Benefits

_____ Poor Claims Service _____ Cancellation by Ins. Co.

Section 2   EMPLOYEE AND DEPENDENT INFORMATION

A. Total Number of Employees . . . . _____
    (Part-time and full-time)

B. Total Number of Full-Time Employees . . . . _____
    (A full-time employee is one who works at least 30 hours per week and 48 weeks
    per year.)

C. Total Number of Eligible Employees . . . . _____
    (Eligible employees are full-time employees who are not waiving this coverage
    due to other group health insurance coverage.)

D. Total Number of Eligible Employees Requesting Medical Coverage . . . . _____
    (The total number of eligible employees requesting medical coverage must be at
    least 75% of all eligible employees **and** at least 60% of all full-time employees.)

E. Is any employee/dependent currently on a continuation of benefits under COBRA
    or State Continuation Law? . . . . Yes_____ No_____
    If Yes, name(s) of individual(s) _____

F. Has any employee/dependent qualified for a continuation of benefits under
    COBRA or State Continuation Law and not yet elected to continue coverage? . . . . Yes_____ No_____
    If Yes, name(s) of individual(s) _____

G. Do you contribute at least 50% of the premium cost of coverage for your employees? . . . . Yes_____ No_____

Waiting period for new employees. **You must choose one** . . . . _____ 30 Days _____ 90 Days

Section 3   COVERAGE INFORMATION

Required

A. Life Insurance and Accidental Death and Dismemberment Insurance (AD&D) is required for **all** Full-Time Employees (including
those waiving medical coverage).

Employee Classification	Amount of Life Insurance	Amount of Weekly Disability Income Insurance (optional)
_____	_____	_____
_____	_____	_____
_____	_____	_____

Deductible   **You must choose one**
B. _____ $250 Deductible
     _____ $500 Deductible

Coinsurance   **You must choose one**
C. _____ 80/20 of $2500 Coinsurance
     _____ 80/20 of $5000 Coinsurance

MET-AP-8   (Continued on back side)   7948-690

Courtesy of Golden Rule Insurance Co.

Section 3   COVERAGE INFORMATION (continued)

Major Medical   **You must choose one**
D. _____   Absolute Value Plus
     _____   Absolute Value Traditional
     _____   Absolute Value Traditional with PCS card

Optional Health Coverage
E. _____   Maternity Benefits -- covered the same as any illness
     _____   Supplemental Accident Benefit
     _____   Weekly Disability Benefits (note amount above in Life Insurance Section)

Optional Dependent Life Insurance
F. _____   Option A -- $1000 spouse and $500 each child
     _____   Option B -- $2000 spouse and $1000 each child

Section 4   REQUESTED EFFECTIVE DATE

Month   Day   Year
The effective date will be the later of the requested effective date or the date this application is received and approved by the Home Office.

Section 5   JOINDER AGREEMENT

The undersigned employer, desiring to obtain the benefits of group insurance for its employees hereby agrees to join one of the Golden Rule Trusts as a Participating or Enrolled Employer. If approved by Golden Rule, the employer accepts and agrees to be bound by the provisions of: (a) the Agreement and Declaration of Trust dated July 30, 1977, as amended, which created this Trust; and (b) the Master Insurance Policy issued to the Trustee by Golden Rule. The Employer understands that the documents referred to in items (a) and (b) are subject to future amendments.

The Employer certifies that the Producer of Record has discussed group eligibility, contribution requirements, participation requirements, pre-certification requirements, provisions for preexisting conditions, and that the Employer fully understands these requirements and provisions.

The Employer understands that the Producer of Record is an independent contractor and not an agent of Golden Rule Insurance Company. The employer understands that the Producer of Record cannot bind coverage, or change or modify conditions of coverage.

The Employer understands that the Underwriting Department of Golden Rule may call the employer and employees at the employer's place of business to develop information to enable Golden Rule to make a prompt underwriting decision.

The Employer understands that Golden Rule has the right to change premiums by class as necessary. Factors include age, sex, claims experience, employee participation, geographic area, and the length of the Employer's participation in the plan.

COMPLIANCE WITH EMPLOYMENT LAWS: I understand and agree that: (a) as an Employer, I may be subject to State and/or Federal Laws mandating specific insurance terms (such as coverage continuation, or sex discrimination in relation to pregnancy benefits); (b) if the insurance benefits I have selected are contrary to any of these laws, I am solely responsible for compliance with these laws, including the payment of any required benefits which are not covered by this insurance; and (c) neither Golden Rule nor the Trustee/Policyholder is acting as plan sponsor or plan administrator, as defined in the Employee Retirement Income Security Act of 1974 (ERISA).

Signed at _____ on ___ / ___ / ___
                                          City   State   Month Day Year

Employer Signature _____

Employer Name _____ Title _____

Section 6   PRODUCER'S STATEMENT

I hereby certify that all of the information herein is complete and correct, that the firm is a bona fide business establishment, and that I know nothing unfavorable about the group. I certify that each employee has completed the employee application with his or her own hand. I further certify that (1) I have complied with all of Golden Rule's rules and requirements, (2) I have explained to and the Employer fully understands the provisions for preexisting conditions and pre-certification, and (3) I have explained to the Employer the requirements for contribution and participation and these requirements are being met. I have instructed the employer to not cancel current group coverage before certificates of insurance have been issued by Golden Rule Insurance Company and delivered by me.

Producer Signature _____ on ___ / ___ / ___
                                                                                          Month Day Year

Producer Name_____

Producer Number _____

Phone Number _____

Courtesy of Golden Rule Insurance Co.

There are three possible scenarios if these questionnaires come back with too many "yes" answers: the coverage may cost you more, one or more of your employees may be denied coverage—or your company may be turned down altogether.

If an answer on a short form indicates a significant health problem, the insurer may require more information. This may include data from the Medical Information Bureau (a kind of "credit bureau" on individual medical histories) indicating whether the applicant has been previously declined coverage, a physician's statement testifying as to the patient's health, a medical exam, or lab work.

Participation: The carrier will want as many of the employees as possible to choose the coverage in order to maximize his ability to cancel out bad risks—unhealthy employees—with good. For example, in a five-person company at least four people should participate; at least six employees should participate in a seven-person company, etc. Otherwise, there's a risk that a disproportionately low number of healthy people will sign up.

In employer-pay-all plans, typically all of the eligible employees must enroll. In group plans of 20 to 49 people in which employees contribute to premium payments, typically 75% of the eligible employees, i.e., full-timers must enroll. If dependent coverage is selected, typically 75% of enrolled employees who have dependents must request that coverage. The insurer should let you off the hook if an employee can prove that he/she has coverage under a spouse's plan.

The insurer also wants to make sure you're genuinely buying the coverage for your employees and not your sick Uncle Fred who is having a tough time getting insurance on his own. Amazing as it may seen, a number of small companies have been involved in this practice.

To be eligible for coverage, the company will typically have to meet the following requirements:

- Each employee must be working at least 30 hours a week.
- They must be bona fide employees, not contractors or consultants.
- If there are five or more participants in the health plan, no more than half of the participants can be related to each other.
- At least two of the employees under the plan must maintain a separate residence.

(There are special rules for self-employed people, which we discuss in Chapter 14.)

How Small Business Rates Are Set

One of the biggest complaints small business leaders voice about buying coverage is that they not only pay a premium price for health insurance, but rates can skyrocket by more than 50% in one year.

While how much you pay depends a great deal on where your business is located, the age and health of your employees, and the practices of your current carrier, it also depends on what kind of rating system your insurer uses. There are moves afoot to make these systems more uniform.

Two rating methods that have generated the most complaints—and which we think small businesses should avoid if they can—are tier and durational rating methods. Similar to an adjustable-rate mortgage on a home, these rate schemes lure in companies with low "teaser" premiums and then subject the company to "rate shock" in future years.

There are moves afoot to take the "tease" out of teaser rates. The National Association of Insurance Commissioners (NAIC) in late 1990 proposed model state legislation that would limit the range between the highest and lowest rates that a company can offer. The proposal would also restrict tier, durational and health status rating. Each state legislature must decide on its own whether to adopt the model law or a version of it.

Until your state legislature decides its policy, we believe that the only circumstance under which you should consider choosing a teaser rate is one in which you have a fallback option should your experience turn sour—a community rated scheme such as the Blues or an HMO that will agree to provide you coverage without extensive underwriting (asking all those nosy questions about your employees' health).

Here is a description of these and other rates and how they are set. An insurer can combine these techniques:

- Community rates
- Age-sex/marital status rating
- Tier rating
- Health status rating
- Durational rating
- Area rating
- Industry rating

Community rates mean that all groups in a community get the same rates for a given product. There are still some Blue Cross/Blue Shield plans and HMOs that offer pure community rates without factoring in adjustments for age or sex. Pure community rating is a good deal for you if your employees and their dependents are older or sicker than average, because they will get the same rates as a company of younger employees. For the same reason, pure community rating is a poor deal if your employees are mostly young and healthy. However, one advantage of community rating with the Blues is that they won't cancel your coverage if your experience turns sour.

Age, sex and marital status rating is just like it sounds. A 60- to 65-year-old man will cost, on average, five or six times more to insure than a 20- to 30-year old man, and women cost more than men at most ages. This system is also combined with the other rating techniques listed here.

Insurers usually slot individuals into five-to-ten-year age bands, so if you employ several 39-year-old employees who are just turning 40, you might have a large rate increase.

Tier rating means that an insurer categorizes a small group into one of several slots based on its claims history. For example, an insurer may have five slots: bad, poor, average, good, and excellent. The excellent groups may get 30% off the average premium, while the bad groups may get hit with an extra 50% charge.

Health status rating sets rates based on the health of each individual in a small group. The insurer could look at the diagnoses of the individual's past claims and judge the likelihood of future claims. The insurer could refuse some individuals insurance, or offer very expensive but limited benefits, or exclude specific conditions from coverage. For example, a diabetic is likely to have large future claims, so he or she may be charged a very high premium or refused coverage. This process may apply to both employees and their spouses and children. However, a person with a health problem who is declined by an insurance company may be accepted by a Blues plan or HMO, perhaps with exclusions.

Durational rating is a method some insurers use to offer low "teaser" rates. If all the individuals in a group have passed the medical underwriting "exam" the group will have rather low claim costs—for the first year. But the insurer knows that the clean bills of health will eventually wear off: illnesses will appear, claims cost will go up, and so the insurer raises its rates after the initial year.

Under durational rating schemes, small businesses are given the option of going through the medical underwriting process again—submitting to questionnaires about their health status—after a few years. If the small group passes, it will get low rates. If not, the rates may go way up. So durational rating is a great deal if you know for certain your employees will never get sick. Would you like to sell us that crystal ball?

Area rating is just as it sounds—setting rates by territory, whether it's a county or a zip code. Usually urban areas are more expensive than rural. Interestingly enough, there's a direct correlation between a high doctor/patient ratio and high rates. If your mailing address is in a city but your operations are in the suburbs, you may be charged the higher city rate. In this case, your agent may be able to get you the lower rate. But don't expect savings of more than a few percentage points.

Industry rating categorizes certain professions and businesses on how "expensive" they are to insure relative to other occupations. We outlined some of them earlier in this chapter. For example, hairdressers and interior decorators in some cities have a higher than average incidence of AIDS and lawyers tend to be expensive to insure because they are more likely to bring a lawsuit if something goes wrong. The phrase "physician, heal thyself" takes on a special significance: Doctors are expensive to insure because they tend to use medical services like they're going out of style.

High-turnover businesses are more expensive to insure because they tend to require a lot of administrative work on the part of the insurer to enroll and de-enroll employees. What's more, the employees who are the sickest and therefore need the coverage are the ones who keep working for the employer.

Although most on-the-job injuries are covered by workers' compensation insurance and not by medical insurance, the expense of coordinating coverage with the workers' comp insurer may add to the medical insurer's cost of dealing with certain industries. And some businesses may have long-term chemical hazards that may cause illness but whose cause can't be proved except in lengthy court cases.

Don't panic if one insurer says it won't provide coverage for your business. Insurer's policies on industry rating vary. Blue Cross/Blue Shield plans often do not exclude any industry. What's more, if your company is large enough, it will generally be able to negotiate special arrangements with insurers.

MULTIPLE EMPLOYER WELFARE ARRANGEMENTS

Some small group medical coverage is provided through Multiple Employer Welfare Arrangements (MEWAs), which are organizations that link together small employers to create a large group for coverage purposes. These organizations, which often aren't associated with insurance companies, typically serve employers with 1 to 25 employees.

Because of federal legislation in the mid-1970s, some MEWAs fall in a gray area between state regulation of insurance and federal regulation of pension and welfare benefit plans.

While many MEWAs are run by reputable companies, including insurers, by the early 1980s enough MEWA problems were surfacing that Congress gave the states their own powers to oversee the plans. Recently, increased federal/state cooperation has helped clarify the primary role the states play in policing MEWAs, particularly the uninsured variety.

Some MEWA organizers contended that the trusts were employee benefit plans and thus protected from state regulation by the Employee Retirement Income Security Act (ERISA). But a 1982 federal law took away the federal preemption for some of them. (Self-funded plans may still be exempt; we'll explain that later.)

Congress thought it had resolved the MEWA issue in 1982. However, "ambiguity over the exact jurisdictional boundaries . . . [allowed] the promoters of fraudulent plans to operate in a twilight world somewhere between state and federal regulations, often playing one set of regulators off against the other. In reality, many of these plans are nothing more than sophisticated pyramid schemes," Sam Nunn (D-Georgia) told a Senate Permanent Subcommittee on Investigation hearing on the MEWA problem in May 1990.

This means that state insurance departments usually are not contacted until problems arise about unpaid claims, by which time the MEWA operators have disappeared, often to reestablish themselves in another state.

The result of this confusion has been a proliferation of health benefits scams that have gone virtually unchecked by either the states or the federal government until fairly recently. No one knows the number of problem MEWAs, however, or even how many MEWAs exist nationwide.

A MEWA may seem to prosper at first because its cash inflow from premiums is greater than its pay-out of claims. But the pay-out is often low on new coverage or new policies and MEWAs that are initially prosperous can quickly founder.

What's more, since they aren't typically set up as insurance companies, they don't have the resources to stay afloat in bad times. Many MEWAs are self-funded, meaning they pay expenses out of the money collected from customers, as opposed to paying them out of reserves. In these cases, there is no well-capitalized insurance company standing behind the promise to pay claims.

MEWAs have left many business owners disillusioned—or worse, broke. For instance, Jo Hardwick, the owner of a real estate agency—a hard-to-insure business—in Cape Coral, Florida, signed herself and some of her employees into a MEWA when she found it difficult to get traditional health insurance. "We paid our premiums and then the problems started," she recalls. Ms. Hardwick says she is out $1,100 in premiums and has had to pay $8,000 in medical bills that were supposed to be covered.

A spate of MEWA abuse scandals has led the U.S. Justice Department and the U.S. Labor Department to initiate criminal investigations. The Department of Labor alone has launched more than 60 investigations. Federal authorities say additional fraud investigations are underway in California, Florida, North Carolina, Pennsylvania, Texas, and other states.

Who's the ultimate loser? In most cases it's the person who files a medical claim, believing he or she has insurance. But it could be the employer. When the claim isn't paid, doctors and hospitals come after him for payment. If the deadbeat carrier were an insurance company, there could be a claim on a state insurance guaranty fund. But these cover only failed conventional insurers, not MEWAs.

The employee pays if he can; if he can't, the health care provider might chalk it up to a bad debt. Adding insult to injury and loss, if the individual has a chronic or acute illness, he may never get coverage of future expenses because insurers may not want to insure him.

The National Association of Insurance Commissioners would like MEWAs to register as third-party administrators in the states so they can be better regulated. North Carolina insurance commissioner James Long, who is also vice chairman of the NAIC, told Nunn that states want a "single, recognized federal agency to which they can turn" and "clear interpretive rules" as to which are state and federal areas of jurisdiction.

Before You Buy

Now that we've told you the horror stories, you're probably wondering if it's worth signing up with a MEWA. Before these agencies or Congress decide who, if anyone, will regulate MEWAs, is there anything you can do?

Here are some tips.

- Press insurance agents/brokers on exactly what they're selling. Some employers complain that insurance agents tell them they are getting coverage from an insurance company when it's really a self-funded MEWA.
- Find out who is really running it—not just processing the claims—and what jobs they've had before.
- Ask for recent audited financial statements for the MEWA.
- Find out who, if anybody, is regulating the MEWA.
- Once in a plan, keep an eye on it.
- Most importantly, stay away from self-insured MEWAs, unless they're run by a sound insurance company. Chances are your state isn't regulating self-insured MEWAs and it's hard to know who the solid operators are. Also be cautious of "partly insured" MEWAs because these only have stop-loss insurance protection against catastrophic experience—assuming they've paid the premiums to an insurer. Don't be misled into thinking that a MEWA's stop-loss insurer is the real guarantee behind the company.

Even insurance agents are wary of selling products of self-insured or partly insured MEWAs, out of fear that they'll be sued if the MEWA collapses.

As for the insured MEWAs? Despite all our horror stories, we think that as long as your agent has done his or her homework, they should be safe.

The premiums will be higher for insured MEWAs, but the peace of mind is worth it, says Michael J. Langan, a vice president with TPF&C's Valhalla, New York office. "In such cases the insurer sponsoring the program has issued a conventional group insurance policy to the multiple employer trust." The premiums are higher because "insured programs have higher expenses due to premium taxes (2-3%) and the costs of including mandated health benefits: up to 20% in some states."

SELF-INSURANCE

If you have more than 75 to 100 employees and a good claims record, you might want to consider self-insurance.

What's self-insurance? It's insurance industry jargon for *not* buying insurance to cope with the smaller medical bills, but getting insurance called "stop-loss" to cover part of the cost of very expensive or numerous claims (although some big companies don't even buy stop-loss). The employer pays an insurance company or a third-party administrator to process the claim forms for the small bills.

A 100-employee company, for example, might buy stop-loss to pay individual claims over $50,000 or the year's aggregate claims above $300,000. The total or "aggregate" limit is usually a certain percentage above the year's expected claim cost.

Self-insurance (also called self-funding) offers companies the following advantages:

- They usually don't have to pay state premium taxes, except on the stop-loss premium.
- They generally don't have to include certain benefits that are mandated under state laws, including everything from drug and alcohol counseling to in-vitro fertilization.
- Cash flow can be improved.
- Administrative costs may be lower.

With stop-loss, companies can limit the risks of self-insurance and budget at the start of each year for the maximum possible claims. Of course, greater protection in the form of lower stop-loss limits costs extra. Experts urge companies to establish their own reserve funds so that an unexpectedly high claim or a drop in cash flow doesn't jeopardize the benefits or leave employees waiting months to be reimbursed for the claim.

Self-Insurance: Examples

Robert Turell, chairman of Los Angeles-based Insurance Design Associates, which sets up self-funding programs for small businesses, claims that by self-funding companies can save between 15% and 20% on their insurance costs.

Companies save money, Turell says, because unlike an insurance company, which charges fees based on a percentage of total claims paid, a benefits administrator usually charges about $10 a month per employee to manage an insurance program. Turell, who has several major law firms as clients, said one company with 250 employees saved about $150,000 a year by partially self-insuring.

Panel Processing, an Alpena, Michigan manufacturer of wood components with 176 employees, cut annual health costs by $60,000 to $70,000 a year by self-funding, as well as instituting other cost management measures in 1986.

The company purchased stop-loss coverage that pays individual claims exceeding $20,000. Aggregate stop-loss coverage kicked in if total claims exceed about $385,000.

Sandmeyer Steel Co., a stainless steel products manufacturer in Philadelphia with 160 employees, is saving between $10,000 and $20,000 a year in costs by self-funding its health care program. "We would rather pay claims as they come in, rather than let an insurance company earn investment income on our premium," pointed out Ron Sandmeyer, vice president of finance and administration of the family-owned business.

In 1984, Sandmeyer's annual claims were about 70% of its premiums, which means that the insurance carrier was keeping 30% of the premiums for administrative expenses and profits. Since an 80% loss ratio is often considered fair, the insurer was keeping more than its share.

Best of all, Sandmeyer doesn't have money tied up in an insurer's reserve account; it got $100,000 back from its previous carrier when it self-insured. Of course a prudent corporation would set up some form of its own reserve for its outstanding claims liability.

While some companies with 75 or more employees self-insure health benefits such as medical, dental, or short-term disability, it's not wise for such small companies to self-insure life insurance, accidental death and dismemberment coverage, or long-term disability coverage because of the risk.

Main Approaches to Self Insurance

Cost plus: A third party pays the claims and bills the employer for the actual amount of claims in a month—the cost—plus an administrative fee.

Administrative services only (ASO): the employer contracts with an insurance company to handle claims and make payments for billed services directly from the employer's bank account.

Self-administration: The employer takes on the risks for claims and does the administrative work itself.

Minimum premium plan: The insurance company provides claims administration services. The employer pays a low initial premium but will be billed for more, up to a limit, if claims experience is high. The insurer may or may not provide stop-loss coverage for an additional fee. This isn't really self-insurance as much as it's an "alternative financing arrangement."

Despite its advantages, a company should not move to self-insure without discussing its risks with a qualified consultant who works in this area. There are many issues to be resolved, including setting up the right size of reserves and the appropriate stop-loss limits, as well as legal and tax matters.

The downside: If a self-funded group has a very large claim and doesn't have stop-loss to cover it, the entire company could be at risk. The company might have to liquidate company assets, says Joyce Wans, vice president of Group Management Services Inc. of Lynnwood, Washington.

Not recommended if: you have fewer than 75 employees. Your medical costs will probably fluctuate too much for self-insurance to work for you.

"Stop-loss premiums are volatile and coverage may not be renewed—it's tricky," says Fred Rumack of Buck Consultants.

Let's use the example of Joe's ten-employee hardware shop. The first year it has almost no claims—$1,000. The following year it has one maternity claim worth $4,000, and a few other claims, for a total of $5,000. So far the cost doesn't seem unmanageable.

The third year, however, there are three more babies—and two of them are Caesarean sections—plus Joe had a coronary. All of a sudden, maternity claims alone shoot up to $16,000, and Joe's claim is $25,000, for a total of over $40,000!

The next year there are no happy or unhappy events, so costs go down to $8,000, a lot of which is still for Joe's coronary.

So, while the average claim over the four years comes out to only $1,350 per employee per year, the cost ranged from $100 to $4,000 per employee. Unless Joe's Hardware has a lot of cash, it would be really hard to budget for that kind of fluctuation.

PURCHASING COALITIONS

When Brad Roller, president and founder of Swiger Coiled Systems, a Cleveland electric motor parts maker, spoke up about the high cost of health insurance for his employees in 1974, he quickly found himself in charge of a plan to help small businesses get affordable coverage.

"We had to do something," Roller said. "Cleveland was the fourth most expensive city in the U.S. for health care."

Under the auspices of the Cleveland Chamber of Commerce's Council of Smaller Enterprises (COSE), small business owners organized themselves into a single group for coverage purposes. Today, COSE contracts with a for-profit third party administrator that performs accounting, enrollment and billing services for the insurance plans and HMOs offered by COSE.

"We save an incredible amount of money," says Roller. Premiums dropped by 15% in 1985, the first full year under the plan, and in the next four years rose by an average of less than 9% annually at a time when increases nationwide were running 20% to 40%.

Some 6,200 small and medium-sized companies participate, covering 46,000 employees and 80,000 dependents. Its current annualized premium is more than $100 million.

The average individual premium is about $180 a month, or $2,160 a year. "That's pretty good for a town where health-care costs are about twice the national average," said John Polk, executive director of COSE.

COSE takes great care in selecting member companies. Those who think they can join to get insurance for a sick employee should think again. "You're not going to sell insurance to somebody whose house is already on fire," said Scott Lynn, who is director of operations for the Council.

Prospective company members are screened for health risks just as they would be if they were buying insurance independently, so their employees are asked about health risks such as cancer, heart disease, and diabetes. Companies can pay one of three rates for coverage depending on how their employees "scored" on the questionnaire: preferred risk, standard, and substandard.

"We keep our rates very competitive," said Lynn—and that's why insurance agents don't "cherry-pick" the low-risk companies away, as is the case with community rated pools.

COSE received national attention in 1992 when then-President George Bush promoted COSE-style coalitions as one cornerstone of his health care reform program. President Bill Clinton has also said that health care coalitions will play a major role in his program. Unlike COSE, however, it seems as though the coalitions that Clinton envisions will be regional community-rated pools.

If you want to find out about any purchasing coalitions in your local area, your best bet is to call your local Chamber of Commerce or the American Hospital Association at (202) 626-2320 and ask for the State Issues Forum. You can also call Scott Lyon of COSE at (216) 621-3300 for ideas on setting one up.

CHAPTER 4
HOW TO SAVE MONEY ON MEDICAL COVERAGE

TRADITIONAL BENEFITS

While we can't offer you a magic formula to cut your health insurance premiums in half, we can show you ways to control your costs. Your first cost-containment effort will take place when you sit down with your insurance agent and will involve eliminating "extras"—riders as they're called in insurance jargon—that sound glitzy but may be of negligible value to your employees. A typical basic insurance plan is reproduced in Figure 4-1.

The second area of cost control, the one that can effect the most dramatic savings, involves containing the size of the doctor and hospital bills themselves and by shifting some of those costs to your employees. These include such cost management techniques as outpatient treatment, pre-admission testing, pre-certification, case management, and flexible benefit programs, and such cost shifting techniques as increasing employee contributions, deductibles and coinsurance payments.

We'll deal with the "extras" on your insurance policy first, some of which are noted in Figure 4-2. Please note: Not all extras are money-wasters; some are money-savers. So we've divided them into two categories: fluffs and possible good buys.

Fluffs

Accident benefit: Under this scheme, deductibles and coinsurance are waived if the injury is due to an accident. This seems to us to be a poor value, and likely duplicated to some extent by the individual's auto insurance.

Alcoholism and drug abuse treatment: The benefit can be for inpatient and/or outpatient treatment of an alcoholism problem. You may not have any choice about buying this coverage if it's mandated by state law. Otherwise these benefits can be expensive because there is very little cost containment in these areas. If you can avoid this benefit, you can still always pay for a "drying-out" clinic when a problem comes up or refer employees to free treatment alternatives such as Alcoholics Anonymous. See Chapter Eleven for more information on drug treatment.

Figure 4-1

Prudential Plus®
90/70

PruCare Plus®
90/70

How A Basic Plan Works

(This is only an example. An actual plan in your area will be similar, but is likely to have different coinsurance, copayment or deductible amounts.)

	Benefit Description and Limits	Network Provider All Services and Supplies Must be Provided or Arranged by Your Personal Physician Plan Pays	Non-Network Provider All Eligible Charges Are Subject to an Annual Deductible Plan Pays
Physician Services	**Office Visits** Includes periodic physical examinations, pap smears, immunizations, injections, well baby care, diagnostic x-ray and lab, chiropractic care, and physical and speech therapy[1]	100% $10 copayment per visit	70% periodic physical exams, immunizations, pap smears, well baby care not covered[7]
	Hospital Visits Includes newborn, surgical procedures, assistant surgeon, anesthesia	90%	70% well baby care not covered
	Maternity Includes pre-natal, delivery, and post-natal care	90% $10 copayment for the first visit	70%
	Inpatient Care For psychiatric, alcohol or drug-related care[2] 30-day maximum per calendar year[3]	90% first 15 days[3] 60% next 15 days[3]	50%
	Outpatient Care For psychiatric, alcohol or drug-related care[2] $2500 maximum annual benefit	100% 1st 3 visits then 70% each visit thereafter	50% $40 per visit maximum benefit
Hospital Services	**Outpatient Care** Emergency room	100% after $25 copayment per visit	70%
	Surgery (services and supplies)		
	Inpatient Care Room and board (semi-private room) Intensive Care, Pre-admission Testing, All Other Hospital Charges	90%	
	Psychiatric, alcohol and drug-related care[2] 30-day maximum per calendar year[3]	90% first 15 days[3] 60% next 15 days[3]	50%
	Well baby care	90%	Not covered
Other Services	Convalescent Nursing Home Care	90% up to 100 days per period of care	70% up to 60 days per period of care
	Psychiatric, alcohol and drug-related care in an Intermediate Care Facility (ICF)[4] 60-day maximum per calendar year[5]	90% first 30 days[5] 60% next 30 days[5]	50% $87.50 per day maximum benefit
	Home Health Care		70% up to 60 visits per calendar year $35 per visit maximum benefit
	Outpatient Private Duty Nursing		70% $7,000 maximum annual benefit
	Hospice Care $7,400 maximum benefit per period of care	90%	
	Ambulance and Chemo/Radiation Therapy		
	Diagnostic x-ray and lab, chiropractic care (other than office visit)		70%
	Physical and Speech Therapy (other than office visit) 90-day maximum per calendar year		
Prescription Drugs (prescribed by network or non-network physician)	**Without Prescription Drug Option**	Plan pays 70% after a separate $50 annual deductible	Plan pays 70% after a separate $50 annual deductible
	With Prescription Drug Option	100% after the lesser of $5 copayment per prescription/refill or dispensing pharmacy's normal retail price	Plan pays 70% after a separate $50 annual deductible
	Annual deductible per calendar year	None	$200 per individual $500 per family
	100% Benefit Feature		After an individual has incurred $10,000 of eligible charges in a calendar year (not including deductible, copayments and any benefits already payable at 100%), the plan pays 100% of remaining eligible charges in that year[6]
	Individual Lifetime Maximum	Unlimited	$1,000,000

[1] Physical and speech therapy each has a 90-day maximum per calendar year.

[2] Psychiatric, alcohol and drug-related care are subject to a $50,000 maximum lifetime benefit. Special state requirements may apply.

[3] If the only stay is in a hospital, then the benefits above apply. Otherwise each two days of Intermediate Care Facilities (ICF) services reduces by one the number of days available for hospital inpatient stays. And each day of a hospital inpatient stay reduces by two the number of days available for ICF services.

[4] Intermediate Care Facility (ICF) treatment means continuous treatment of not less than three hours and not more than twelve hours in a 24-hour period. It does not include a hospital inpatient stay.

[5] If the only stay is in an Intermediate Care Facility, then the benefits above apply. Otherwise each two days of Intermediate Care Facility services reduces by one the number of days available for hospital inpatient stays. And each day of a hospital inpatient stay reduces by two the number of days available for ICF services.

[6] Eligible charges for outpatient psychiatric, alcohol and drug-related care will not increase to 100%, but will continue to be paid at the percentages shown in this Benefit Summary. However, the 50% and the 70% Outpatient charges in excess of the deductible will count toward the $10,000.

[7] Special state requirements may apply. For specific benefits, refer to the Plan Benefit Summary for your area or contact Member Services.

All benefits are subject to Coordination of Benefits.

Figure 4-2

Non-Health Care Group Coverages

Here's A Summary of Small Group Non-Health Care Coverages Available

Benefits Available	Amounts Available	BENEFIT PLANS AVAILABLE	
		Flat Plans	**Earnings Plans**
Employee Term Life Insurance (Required on all plans.)	Minimum Per Employee 1-Life Plan—$25,000 per 2 or more lives—$10,000 per employee Maximum Per Employee EBP plans—$50,000 Group plans—$100,000	Each employee will have the same fixed amount of insurance regardless of earnings or position in the company.	Amount determined by employee's annual earnings. The plan may provide either: 1 Times earnings 1½ Times earnings 2 Times earnings
Weekly Disability Income (Available on plans covering 2 or more lives)	Minimum Amount: $50 Maximum Amount: $500 but not to exceed 70% of an employee's weekly earnings.	Each employee will have the same fixed amount of insurance regardless of earnings or position in the company.	The weekly benefit amount may be 50%, 60% or 70% of employee weekly earnings.
Accidental Death and Dismemberment Insurance (Optional on EBP Plans. Required on Group Plans).	Either equal to or twice the amount of Employee Term Life Insurance.		
Dependent Term Life Insurance (Optional)	Spouse: Either $1,000 or $2,000 Children: $1,000 ultimate amount		

EBP (4 – 19 lives) DENTAL				GROUP (20 + lives)			
(Available if four or more employees are insured for healthcare coverage)				FREEDOM OF CHOICE DMO (Available on Group plans with 20 + eligible employees)	GROUP DENTAL (Available on Freedom of Choice DMO Plans as the Alternate Plan)		
Deductible	Then Plan Pays	Dental Plan Maximum		DMO Network Plan Pays	Deductible	Then Plan Pays	Dental Plan Maximum
None	100%		**Preventive Services** • exams • certain x-rays • cleaning of teeth	100%	None	100%	
$50 Lifetime deductible	80%	$800 per person first benefit year; $1600 per person thereafter	**Basic Services (Restorative)** • simple extractions • most periodontal treatment • fillings • most root canal treatment • routine oral surgery	100%	$50 Calendar Year deductible	100% up to Scheduled Limits	$1,000 per person per calendar year
			Basic Services (Specialty) • osseous surgery • molar root canal therapy • removal of impacted teeth • general anesthesia	50%			
$50 Benefit Year deductible	50%		**Major Services** • crowns • bridges • partial dentures • inlays • dentures	50%		50%	
$50 Deductible per treatment plan		$1,200 Lifetime per person	**Orthodontia (Not available on EBP plans under 10 lives)** Orthodontic treatment is available as an optional benefit. Coverage is for dependent children age 19 or less.	50%	$50 Deductible per treatment plan		$1,000 Lifetime per person

EBP/GRP 859 Ed. 7-89
The Prudential Insurance Company of America
Corporate Office: Newark, N.J. 07101
Litho in U.S.A. by PruPress

Alternative medicine: Alternative medicine, such as acupuncture and homeopathy, has its adherents, but it is also a fertile ground for fraud. With the exception of chiropractic medicine, we'd recommend against paying money for this coverage. (Unless you're unfortunate enough to do business in one of those states where coverage of such treatments is mandated by the state legislature, an issue we'll deal with in Chapter Fifteen.)

Ambulance: Ambulances are a low-cost item, unless an air ambulance is used for something elaborate such as organ transplants or to fly one of your employees home from a skiing vacation in Austria. If you want to save a few pennies per employee per month, this is one benefit that can be eliminated.

Cash benefits: These benefits pay a flat amount for each day the employee stays in the hospital over and above the coverage you have. Avoid it. Your sick-pay program should serve this purpose, and the cash payments are usually so small they amount to pocket change.

Dread disease: Or, your employee "hits the jackpot" and receives coverage *if* he, she, or a covered dependent happens to be "lucky" enough to contract a specified condition, such as cancer or tuberculosis. As if cancer deserves the benefit and double pneumonia doesn't! Avoid this coverage like the plague.

Executive checkups: This is usually an overpriced perk for executives. Fancy executive checkups are probably worth no more than an ordinary routine physical. What's more, "typically these benefits are taxable to the executives eligible for this benefit because not all employees are entitled to receive it," says William H. Dearth Jr., an actuary with Martin E. Segal Co. in West Palm Beach, Florida.

Podiatric care: If this is an optional benefit, it may be overpriced and it's probably something you can do without. Some insurers and employers have accused podiatrists of ordering excessive X-rays or recommending expensive therapies. So the cost of this coverage may not be worth the benefit to your employees' feet.

Routine physicals: Annual exams simply aren't necessary for younger employees. The employees who benefit the most from these health screening sessions are often the older employees, who are probably the best able to pay for it themselves. If you're a believer in preventative medicine, the best approach is probably an HMO, which often includes physicals as part of its benefit package.

Possible Good Buys

Chiropractic benefit: While the verdict isn't in from the medical community on how chiropractic works or whether it works, scores of people with back problems swear by it. Sometimes it's a cheap alternative to orthopedic surgery.

But be careful. "Chiropractic care is widely believed to be the one of the most abused kinds of care. It should only be provided using strict guidelines on cost and duration," says Bryan Lane, an actuary with TPF&C in Stamford, Connecticut.

Dental Care: This benefit may or may not be a fluff. Of all areas of medical care, preventative dentistry (i.e., regular checkups) effectively reduces expensive treatments later on.

On the other hand, if you choose not to offer dental coverage, your employees can probably afford to pay for many of the most expensive procedures. With the possible exception of orthodontia and periodontal disease (gum disease), dental costs aren't exactly catastrophic compared to treating a heart attack or even a broken leg.

The best way to approach a dental benefit is by using cost control. There are two approaches. The first is to set up a flexible spending account (explained more below) that will enable employees to funnel pre-tax dollars into dental and other expenses. The second is to join a dental PPO or an HMO that offers dental care (explained in a different chapter), in which your employees can enjoy significant savings over the usual costs. Ask your insurance broker what's available in your area.

Some health benefit experts prefer dental programs through an HMO to dental PPOs. "Dental PPOs offer price discounting but there's no volume of service control; the dentist is still in control of the total cost. HMOs offer control on price *and* volume because they're prepaid," says Bryan Lane of TPF&C.

Mental health: Often these benefits are mandated for insurance policies by state law, as drug and alcoholism treatment frequently is. If they aren't, this may be an important benefit, since there aren't free therapy alternatives. Be choosy about the coverage, however. You'll pay dearly if the mental health benefits are a blank check for the shrink, and the results may not be measurable. Two suggestions: HMOs may offer effective, lower-cost coverage. And look for programs that feature social workers and clinical psychologists on the staff in addition to psychiatrists, since these professionals don't command the same high fees.

Vision care: This benefit usually pays for eye exams and glasses or contact lenses. (Diseases of the eye, on the other hand, will be covered under your regular plan.) There are usually limits on the reimbursement for lenses, frames, and contact lenses.

For small businesses, this benefit is usually not a good deal because it's going to be expensive. This is due to a phenomenon called adverse selection, the likelihood that a disproportionate number of unhealthy people, or those likely to use coverage, will sign up for coverage. Typically only those companies with lots of employees who need the benefit buy the coverage—so there is no subsidy by those who don't need the benefit—i.e., those with 20-20 eyesight! What's more, the benefit is of questionable value because the cost of glasses and exams is usually small enough for individuals to budget.

As with dental coverage, there are a couple of ways to make this benefit work more effectively. First, you can set up a flexible spending account (explained later in this chapter) so your employees can fund their vision (or other) care with pre-tax dollars. Second, you can provide the coverage through an HMO or optical care PPO since these setups often don't feature the same high markups on glasses and contact lenses.

Birthing center benefit: This pays for deliveries in a "friendlier" setting than an operating room. This is a good deal as long as it costs nothing extra, since birthing centers should be no more expensive than a traditional operating room approach, and the benefit may be good public relations for the employees.

Extended care/convalescent care: This benefit pays for recovery outside the hospital. This benefit shouldn't cost much extra (it may save money for the insurer) because it replaces expensive hospital bed-days with time in a cheaper skilled nursing facility or in the patient's home. This is not a long term care benefit for conditions such as Alzheimer's disease.

Hospice care: This is treatment of terminally ill patients in which the goal is to provide maximum comfort instead of a cure. Hospice care can be rendered in the patient's own home. This benefit may not cost anything extra because it replaces expensive hospital treatment with less expensive hospice treatment. This may also be considered by employees to be a valuable benefit.

Outpatient treatment incentive: Sometimes the plan's usual deductible or coinsurance (out-of-pocket payment) is waived for outpatient treatment in order to encourage it as an alternative to more costly hospital inpatient treatment. If so, you probably shouldn't pay extra for the waiver feature.

COST CONTAINMENT FOR TRADITIONAL BENEFITS

Usual, Customary, and Reasonable

Even though it may not seem that way, insurers have never been interested in giving doctors carte blanche to charge whatever they want. Insurers calculate payments based on "usual, customary, and reasonable" (UCR) charges, or they have a fixed schedule that assigns a dollar limit to these charges.

In brief, insurers or Blues plans make these calculations based on prevailing fees in a geographic area for each procedure or service. Sometimes these formulas are fairly elaborate and profile the charge levels of individual physicians, and they are updated regularly to compensate for inflation.

Unfortunately, UCR (or R&C—reasonable and customary, as it's sometimes called) doesn't prevent doctors from ordering more services. Doctors may also simply increase their fees, so a fee that used to be considered excessive grows to be "reasonable and customary." Fee schedules go out of date quickly due to inflation, so they have to be adjusted frequently or they are a poor value.

So insurers have had to develop different cost containment techniques in an attempt to keep their customers satisfied. Some of these simply *shift costs* to the employee (make the employee pay more), while others actually attempt to use *cost management* (make the doctors and hospitals accept less, choose a less expensive treatment, or perform only necessary treatments) to make medical care more cost-effective. Here's a rundown of cost-shifting and the cost management techniques.

Making the Employee Pay for Part of the Cost

Contributory plan: One of the simplest ways to reduce your costs is to make the employee pay for some part of the insurance premium. This is called a contributory plan. A good way to do this is to set up a flexible spending account so that the employee's contribution is from pre-tax dollars. This is described later in this chapter in the section called Flexible Benefits.

A study of health insurance coverage among small businesses from 1986 to 1988, performed for the National Association for the Self-Employed by Lewin/ICF, shows that both large and small businesses have contributory plans. Interestingly enough, despite the fact that small business is always characterized as tight-fisted when it comes to benefits, the numbers seem to show that smaller companies are more generous spenders than their larger counterparts, at least when it comes to dependent coverage.

Figure 4-3

PERCENTAGE OF COST PAID BY EMPLOYER

Number Of Employees

	1-9	10-24	25-99	100-499	500+
EMPLOYEE COVERAGE	89%	90%	84%	84%	87%
DEPENDENT COVERAGE	87%	76%	65%	69%	67%

Contributory plans often require a larger contribution for family coverage than for coverage of the employee himself or herself.

The contribution is usually the same amount per month for each employee, though it may also vary by individual as a certain percentage of each employee's pay or premium.

One problem with contributory plans is that most of your employees must agree to participate and pay. Otherwise an insurer will refuse to cover your company in order to avoid adverse selection.

Increasing employee contributions is one technique that works no matter what kind of benefit you have, whether traditional coverage, an HMO, or a PPO.

Deductibles and Copayments

With deductibles, the employee pays a certain dollar amount out of pocket before the insurance kicks in, ranging from $50 to over $1,000. Most deductibles pertain to a year's worth of treatment, but sometimes they apply to individual treatments or conditions.

A copayment—not to be confused with coinsurance—is a form of deductible which is often applied to prescription drugs or physician visits. The insured may be responsible for the first $2 to $10 of each prescription or other service.

Are deductibles effective in controlling costs? It's argued that they eliminate small "nuisance" claims, which can be expensive to the insurance company, since the administrative expense of handling them is high. Deductibles probably encourage some individuals to forgo non-urgent elective treatment. And, of course, if the employee pays part of the bill, the employer's cost will go down.

Experts say that as long as you aren't implementing draconian deductible measures, you can successfully discourage unnecessary medical claims. A Rand Corporation study of health-cost management found that participants who were required to pay a $100 deductible used the health plan 19% less than those who paid no deductible. Those who paid a $500 deductible cut usage 27% compared with those with no deductible; and those who paid a $1,000 deductible cut usage by 39%.

The Rand study also contends that participants didn't compromise their health by using medical services less. After five years of tracking the health status of 8,000 people in the study, no significant health differences were found between groups that used the most health services and those who used the least.

On the other hand, some contend that raising deductibles by $200 or $500 could severely hurt many lower-paid employees because doing so discourages lower-paid employees in particular from seeking medical treatment.

Coinsurance

Another cost-shifting technique is coinsurance, which simply means that the employee pays a percentage of the *eligible* bill after the deductible has been met; 10% to 20% is typical. To protect employees from financial hardship from huge medical bills, most plans specify an out-of-pocket maximum that would be spent by the covered employee, after which the insurer would pay 100% of the bill. Calendar year out-of-pocket maximums are typically $1,000 to $2,000 for each person.

Like deductibles, coinsurance does discourage some excessive use of services because it tends to encourage employees and their dependents to avoid elective treatment. On the other hand, the out-of-pocket protection means that there's really no incentive for cost-containment for long-term stays.

Cost-Sharing Choices

Suppose you wanted to lower your medical insurance costs by 10%. There are two easy ways to do this. You could require your employees to contribute a salary deduction equivalent to 10% of the cost of the program. Or you could increase the deductible and coinsurance to lower the cost by 10%. Or you could do a combination of both.

Deductibles are less "democratic" than contributions because the chances are good that not everyone in the plan will spend enough on health care bills to reach the deductible limit; some employees will have virtually no expenses in a year. The unlucky, sicker ones will wind up bearing more of the cost.

On the other hand, one thing to remember about contributory (salary deduction) plans is that there is a danger that some employees will decline to participate at all, which could cause your company to fall below the insurer's minimum participation requirements. This is especially likely if each employee has to contribute the same amount independent of age, since the younger employees may resent subsidizing the older employees.

So you're walking a tightrope—you want to save as much money as you can but you don't want to make the costs so high that your employees opt out altogether. What's more, employees who opt out will be responsible for their own bills, and may fall into financial trouble if they get sick or injured, creating a moral dilemma on your part regarding whether or not to bail out the employee.

Here are some other factors to weigh:

- Introducing an employee contribution through a salary deduction may complicate your payroll system.
- Both contributions and deductibles/coinsurance will be easier for employees to swallow if they can pay them with pre-tax dollars. See our discussion of flexible spending accounts in the Flexible Benefits section below.

Recommendations: Get feedback from your employees on their needs and tolerance levels. Then strike a balance between employee contributions and the deductible/co-insurance level through a two step process, starting with employee contributions and increasing the deductible or decreasing coinsurance if necessary. Your broker can give you deductible/coinsurance combinations that will lower your cost by various amounts. Then get feedback from employees again. Remember that deductibles and contributions should increase each year with inflation.

Coordination of Benefits

Coordination of benefits (COB) rules are strict standards used by insurance companies to decide who pays for expenses incurred by an individual covered by two or more plans. This usually occurs when a husband and wife each have family coverage from their respective employers. COB prevents "double dipping," getting reimbursed by two insurers for more than the total bill.

There are different ways to coordinate benefits. Depending on how generous you want to be, the employee or dependent can get reimbursed for virtually all of his expenses or very little beyond what one coverage provides. Ask your broker about the different options available for COB.

In circumstances of double coverage you can literally "buy out" the spouse that works for your company so you're no longer paying for his or her coverage. Here's the good news! You can save a lot of money if you adopt the "buy-out" scenario.

Be sure to communicate your efforts clearly. You don't want to appear to be leaving your employee out in the cold. On the one hand, if your employee's spouse is covered under a richer plan than yours (likely if the spouse works for a larger company where benefits are sometimes more generous), you may have a relatively easy time convincing your employee to opt out. On the other hand, your employee might perceive that a valuable benefit is being lost, since double coverage will often fill in gaps in both spouses' and the children's coverage.

You should also share the savings with employees. If an employee agrees to opt out of your plan and settle for dependent coverage under his or her spouse's plan, you should split the savings with your employee. Your broker can help you calculate an incentive that's generous enough to convince employees to opt out, but not so generous that you might be paying more than the cost of their coverage!

You will also want the employee to fill out forms which provide proof of coverage under the spouse's plan. You want to ensure that the individual indeed has coverage elsewhere and can "opt back in" to your plan in the event that the spouse loses his or her job. You also don't want to be penalized by your insurer (i.e., lose your coverage) by falling under the "minimum participation requirements" if many employees choose to opt out.

Cost Management

Cost management seeks to direct patients to use more appropriate and less costly medical treatments. Examples are pre-certification programs, second opinion programs, encouraged outpatient treatment, individual case management, and utilization review. These techniques are fairly standard among insurers today, and offer some savings in cost. Sometimes these programs are offered as "negative riders" which reduce the group's rate. If you are offered these programs as an option, we recommend taking them.

As a practical matter, many insurers have established free "800" hotlines to help patients and their doctors follow the rules. Make sure your insurer has such a number and make sure your employees know how to use the program.

Pre-certification programs: These programs require employees and their dependents to get prior approval from the insurer for many kinds of non-emergency treatment. The plan of treatment from the doctor would be scrutinized by medical specialists who question whether a treatment is necessary or can be performed less expensively. For example, if a doctor planned to hospitalize someone for two days for cataract surgery, the insurer would probably ask why the procedure couldn't be done on an outpatient basis.

Mandatory Second Opinion Programs Some insurers specify that all non-emergency surgery must be subject to second opinions. Others specify a list of procedures. Here is a list of procedures which are often part of second opinion programs:

- Tonsillectomy and adenoid removal
- Hysterectomy
- Hernia repair
- Hemorrhoid removal
- Knee surgery
- Removal of gall bladder
- Removal of prostate
- Spinal or disc surgery
- Varicose vein surgery
- Caesarean section

These are surgical procedures that are often performed unnecessarily. If a doctor recommends one of these procedures to the insured on a non-emergency basis, the patient has to get the opinion of another physician—and the insurer usually picks up the tab. If the doctors disagree, the patient is usually free to choose whether or not to have the procedure done. If the patient doesn't get the second opinion, there is a penalty which can range from non-payment for the operation to an extra out-of-pocket payment.

Encouraged outpatient treatment: Many surgical procedures can be performed safely and efficiently on an outpatient basis. This means that the patient does not have to spend any nights in the hospital. Here is a list of operations which are often subject to outpatient programs:

- Arthroscopy
- Dilation and curettage
- Endoscopic exams
- Hernia repair
- Tonsillectomy

Large Case Management: Very serious and complicated medical cases can often be handled better by going outside the rules of the medical benefits plan. For example, recuperation from or treatment of some serious illnesses may best be done in the patient's home if nursing care and monitoring equipment are available. Some of the conditions in which home treatment is sometimes appropriate are low birth weight babies, spinal and head injuries and organ transplants. Even if the patient's coverage may not include home treatment costs, the insurer who performs large case management would probably evaluate whether bending the rules will save the insurer money and the give the patient a better benefit at the same time.

Utilization review: Insurers hire agencies to look at the appropriateness of procedures, length of hospital stays, and so on.

Pre-admission testing: Some doctors customarily admit patients into a hospital the day before a non-emergency operation in order to have the hospital perform the required blood tests and X-rays. At room and board of $500 to $1,000 per day, this seems like a high price for a lousy hotel, to say the least! To counter this practice it is common for policies to require patients to have their testing done as an outpatient when possible instead of staying overnight before non-emergency surgery is performed.

As with the second opinion and outpatient programs, make sure the insurer has an free "800" number to call, and make sure your employees know the rules.

COST CONTAINMENT FOR ALTERNATIVE DELIVERY SYSTEMS

By their very nature, HMOs and PPOs try to incorporate many of the cost management techniques described above. There is also some flexibility for the employer to add benefits for better coverage or to remove benefits to lower costs.

One of the traditional attractions of HMOs was that office visits and routine check-ups were free. This is still the case for some HMOs, but it's expensive for the HMO to cater to those subscribers who in insurance jargon "overutilize" the benefits. Many HMOs now require the patient to put down some cash in the form of copays for certain kinds of services. They may also trim costs by not offering some benefits such as vision care. Employee salary deductions can also be used to help pay for HMO and PPO costs.

LIMITING RETIREE COVERAGE

Until recent years, taking care of retirees wasn't costly since Medicare picked up most of the bills of these individuals after age 65 and early retirement programs weren't yet commonplace. However, the increasing popularity of early retirement options—ironically, a cost-containment measure in itself—has driven retirement costs up dramatically. In addition, "Medicare has implemented cost containment features which have shifted medical costs from Medicare to employer sponsored retiree plans," says actuary William Dearth of Martin E. Segal & Co.

Corporate America's total liability for retiree health benefits was pegged at a whopping $402 billion in 1989, including $175 billion in benefits that aren't earned yet, according to the federal General Accounting Office, the investigative arm of Congress.

New accounting rules promulgated by the Financial Accounting Standards Board, the self-regulatory body overseeing the accounting profession, will increase the accounting costs of these programs dramatically. The rules require employers to measure the expected future costs of retiree medical benefits as a liability on their balance sheets and to expense a portion of those costs on their income statements. Currently, employers ignore the future liability and report only the pay-as-you-go costs of the retiree medical programs.

With the new rules, there is less incentive for employers to offer retiree health benefits because there is currently little opportunity for tax breaks on prefunding these benefits, as there is with pension plans. The rules affect virtually every company except government bodies and charitable organizations. Non-government employers with more than 500 workers will have to comply with them by 1993 and smaller employers by 1995.

If you do offer retiree medical benefits, you should know that insurers offer products which complement Medicare benefits to cover retirees who are 65 and over. If you are providing retiree benefits, tell your insurer who your retirees are because these products are usually less expensive than comparable standard coverage.

Caution: If you're considering terminating these benefits, be sure to get expert legal advice. Some courts have decided that retiree health benefits are contractual promises to existing retirees the same way defined benefit pension plans are and may not be discontinued or altered.

FLEXIBLE BENEFITS

Michigan Spring, a 100-employee Muskegon, Michigan spring maker, discovered in 1980 that its benefits were tailored to a family makeup that was dominant when "Leave It to Beaver" was on prime time TV—young male employees with a nonworking spouse and two children—although few of its employees fit that description.

Since the work force included single women, employees with working spouses, single parents, and people nearing retirement, they decided to throw out their cookie-cutter health plan and replace it with one which could be tailor-made to employees' individual needs.

Flexible benefit plans, in which participants can choose some or all of their benefits, are probably the fastest growing benefit option adopted by employers. A Hewitt Associates survey showed that a total of 1,001 flexible benefit programs were expected to be in effect as of January 1, 1990, compared with a mere 19 in 1981.

Flexible benefits aim to allow employees to choose the benefits they want and can be designed to have the added advantage of allowing individuals to pay for many of them out of pre-tax dollars. The choices can be twofold: among different levels of one benefit and/or among different benefits.

These plans may typically include two or more health plans, other benefit plans, and one or two reimbursement accounts out of which employees can pay themselves back on a pre-tax basis for certain out-of-pocket health care or dependent care expenditures. But these benefits come at a price—meeting the Internal Revenue Code standards.

The Cafeteria Plan

A *cafeteria plan* is a flexible benefit plan that allows the employee a choice between cash (or certain other taxable benefits) and nontaxable benefits (such as health insurance). Cafeteria plans are regulated by Section 125 of the Internal Revenue Code. They can be funded by employer contributions, employee contributions, or both.

There are several different ways to design a cafeteria plan. Under some designs, some of the benefits are required. Other designs limit employee choices to different packages of benefits. Also, employer contributions may be made in real dollars or in "credits."

These are the benefits that can be offered in a cafeteria plan:

- Health insurance
- Group life insurance
- Disability coverage
- Dental and vision coverage
- Dependent care assistance (day care)
- Medical reimbursement plans for non-insured expenses, possibly including doctor visits to the optometrist, gynecologist or pediatrician, along with deductibles, coinsurance
- 401(k) plans (a retirement plan we'll talk about later)
- Vacation days

Cafeteria plans can't include education assistance benefits and other fringe benefits, whether or not they're taxable.

Flexible Spending Account

A *flexible spending account* is one type of cafeteria plan that allows an employee to choose between receiving taxable cash or pretax reimbursement of certain expenses. Flexible spending accounts can use pre-tax dollars from an employee's salary to pay for certain medical care or dependent care expenses.

For example, if an employee pays $400 a month for day care, he can elect to have his salary reduced and put this amount into the dependent care account. Each month the employee submits a claim and is reimbursed for the $400 which he has paid to the day care center.

For another example, if an employee in the 28% tax bracket normally contributes $50 each month for medical insurance, putting that contribution into a flexible spending account means his pay is really only reduced $36 a month. To look at it another way, instead of paying $600 a year, the employee effectively only pays $432. So you're giving the employee an extra $168 at Uncle Sam's expense.

Federal Tax Treatment

Federal tax treatment of the flexible spending account or cafeteria plan is the same as for other employee benefit costs: Employer contributions are tax deductible to the employer and are not subject to income tax for the employee. Most but not all states follow the federal tax treatment for state income taxes.

Both employers and employees save tax dollars with salary reduction reimbursement accounts. Employers and employees don't pay Social Security (FICA) tax on the amount of elective salary reduction unless the amounts are contributed to 401(k) plans. Likewise employers don't pay federal unemployment tax (FUTA) tax on the amount of salary reduction unless the amounts are contributed to 401(k) plans. Employers may also save on workers' compensation costs and state unemployment taxes.

Rules to follow: The IRS has several rules for you to follow to make sure that the flex plan is "fair" to all of your employees and also to limit employee changes. A few of the more important requirements are listed below.

- No more than 25% of the tax-favored benefits can go to "key" employees, defined as a) owning more than 5% of the company, b) officers earning more than $45,000, or c) owning 1% or more of the company AND earning more than $150,000. Before you institute a program, you should determine whether this discrimination test is likely to cause any problems. Generally, companies with 25 or more employees are less likely to violate these rules than smaller companies.
- Employees can't change their minds about their selections after the start of the plan year unless there's a change in the family status and the new selections have to be related to that alteration in family status. In other words, an employee could add a child care benefit as a result of a birth in the family but couldn't add a 401(k) retirement plan. Here are the allowed changes in family status:

    Marriage
    Divorce
    Death of a spouse or child
    Birth or adoption of a child (pregnancy doesn't count)
    Termination of a spouse's employment
    The spouse switches from part-time to full-time employment—or vice versa.

- Unused credits or benefits, including unused vacation days, can't be carried over to a subsequent year.

- Funds allocated to one flexible spending account, such as a health care reimbursement account, can't be used to reimburse other types of claims, such as dependent care expenses.
- Employees can only withdraw money from their reimbursement accounts if they can prove they had a bona fide medical expense or dependent care expense. For example, the employee can submit a receipt from the doctor or day care center, or an insurer's explanation of benefits form showing that a deductible was paid. The employee must certify that the claim has not been reimbursed through any other coverage or, in the case of dependent care, that the charge is a reimbursable expense under the plan.

Who sets up flex plans: You can either hire an outside firm to administer the plan or buy software to handle enrollment, benefit payments and record keeping. Some insurers also offer administrative services for flex plans. Ask your broker.

Is instituting a flex plan going to cost a lot of money? Not necessarily, according to Weber Lipshie, a New York accounting firm that designs many of these plans for small business. You can pay to administer the plan out of the savings you'll gain by not paying the social security tax on the reduced salaries.

The Verdict on Flex Plans:

Here is a summary of the advantages and disadvantages of flex plans:

Pluses to employers: Employers can limit their dollar contribution to health insurance benefits rather than automatically raise their contribution as plan costs rise. Creating a flex plan often gives the "aura" of benefit improvements and makes employee contributions more flexible.

Pluses to employees: Employees can receive more benefit value because they can tailor their benefits to their needs. Employees can change benefits as their lives change—for example, when they marry or divorce, as their salaries increase, or as their children mature and leave home.

Drawbacks to employers:

- If the employee incurs a big medical bill and doesn't have enough money to cover it in his account, the employer must nonetheless reimburse the employee right away up to the total annual contribution the employee would make to his medical reimbursement account. Many companies are now trying to decide if they can absorb the added financial risk or whether they should modify the plans or even drop them because of this requirement.
- Some companies are adjusting by lowering the cap for employee contributions to the medical account to $1,000 from $5,000, the typical limit. Companies in industries that have high turnover may require new employees to work for a certain period of time before they become eligible to participate.

- The flex plan could result in "adverse selection" that could ultimately increase costs. For example, if an employee knows she's going to have a baby in 1992, she may opt for the enriched medical benefit. One way around adverse selection is to limit the difference in benefits between the high and low options.
- Flex plans aren't do-it-yourself operations; they require professional tax and design advice as well as administration and excellent employee communications.

Recommendations on Flex Plans

Which businesses should consider flexible benefits: Usually one with at least 25 employees, although companies with as few as ten have implemented these accounts. Why the cutoff? For one thing, smaller companies have to worry about "top-heavy" rules, serving up too much of the benefit "pie" to highly compensated employees.

Secondly, these plans may be more expensive for small companies to run. You may have to hire a consultant or someone from a CPA firm to help you set up the program and keep it running, although a few insurance companies are starting to market these plans to small companies. You will also have to have a human resources/payroll system that can keep track of the accounts.

Thirdly, as we mentioned earlier in our chapter about insurance rates, you may not have the option to customize a flex plan as a small business person because it's not cost-effective for insurers to custom tailor a plan for such a small group.

Recommendations for "larger" small employers: If you decide to go with a flex plan, it's important to have an excellent employee communications program because choosing from a "menu" of benefits can be confusing to employees who may be used to having their benefits "spoon-fed."

For example, Michigan Spring phased in their plan over a two-year period. They used payroll envelope stuffers to explain the concept. They asked the employees to take the package home, review the benefits and discuss the options with their family members.

During the first year of Michigan Spring's program, nearly all workers retained their original benefits packages. During the second year, many employees elected to save money by choosing higher deductibles, and opted to use less-expensive care such as outpatient surgery—or decided against elective treatment altogether—a pattern that continued.

Much of the success was attributable to the communications program, said Michigan Spring general manager Thomas Wheeler. "We were very up front with employees," he explained. "We told them that if we worked together to contain costs, the company would remain competitive and we would share the savings."

Strategies for smaller small employers: If you want to implement a flex plan, we recommend that you start simple. First offer salary reductions for flexible spending accounts as a way to fund employee contributions to the medical plan and other medical expenses and dependent care. Later you can also add a 401(k) plan (an employee-funded retirement plan, explained later) or incorporate your existing one once the flex plan gets going. You can also add options for life insurance and disability insurance.

We also recommend that small businesses stick with the reimbursement accounts and salary reductions for employee contributions but avoid offering the different medical plan options because you confront adverse selection—the phenomenon that employees tend to choose the benefits they plan to "use."

BEND YOUR STATE LEGISLATOR'S EAR

The best prospect for keeping insurance rates under control is for small business owners to convince their elected representatives—especially on the state level, where insurance rates are regulated—to pass laws that help small businesses get affordable coverage. There are three ways to accomplish this: by stabilizing rates for small groups, limiting the circumstances under which insurers can cancel them, and exempting small businesses from having to buy coverage that includes expensive "bells and whistles," or unnecessary coverage. (The other term for "bells and whistles" is "mandated benefits.")

In Chapter Sixteen we provide a comprehensive breakdown of the states that have already passed or are considering such legislation. The list is impressive. Check to see if your state is considering such legislation. If not, get your state senator or representative on the case.

Here is a summary of the states that have passed laws and those where legislation is under consideration:

States that have passed legislation permitting small businesses to buy no-frills coverage: Connecticut, Florida, Illinois, Kansas, Missouri, Rhode Island, Virginia, Washington.

States considering legislation to permit the purchase of no-frills coverage: Arizona, California, Maryland, Montana, New Mexico, New York, North Dakota, Ohio and Tennessee.

States considering legislation to stabilize rates for small business: Indiana, Iowa, Maine, Nebraska, New Hampshire, New Mexico, New York, North Carolina, South Carolina, South Dakota and Wisconsin.

CHAPTER 5

THE CARE AND FEEDING OF YOUR MEDICAL BENEFITS

This section is about the ongoing relationship (or lack of it) with your insurance company: matters such as paying bills, changing insurers, what to do when your rates go up. It will also deal with questions employees may bring to you if they have problems understanding their bills or their coverage.

QUESTIONS ABOUT RATES

Q: Do I have to pay my insurance premiums monthly in advance?

For small groups, most insurers will require a monthly premium payment before each month. The payment can either be by mail or via direct debit, in which the premium is automatically deducted from the business' bank account each month.

Q: Is there a grace period for late payments?

Most insurers won't cancel the policy right away if you're late with the payment. The grace period is usually one month and there may be an interest or late charge applied.

Q: What happens if I add new employees or lose them?

Your insurance agent will want to know about all changes in covered employees as soon as possible so that premiums can be adjusted when coverage starts. Because there is a high "dropout" rate among new employees, many insurers require a waiting period before allowing an employee to join the group scheme.

Here's the other reasons why your insurer is interested about your company's change in size: the larger a small business grows, the more likely it is to get a wider choice of benefits, more favorable rates, or more favorable payment arrangements. Alternatively, once a business falls below a certain size, its benefit choices may be restricted, its financial options limited, and the group may even be cancelled.

Q: How often will the rates change?

Medical insurance rates customarily increase annually. However, many insurers reserve the right to change rates with one month's notice.

Q: What are my options when the rates go up?

You can kick the dog, tear up the bill or chew out your agent. In all seriousness, for reasons we outlined in earlier chapters, there's not much you can do about single-digit or low double-digit rate increases because it's simply a reflection of the cost of providing insurance coverage, given medical inflation and the volatile nature of the small business market. On the other hand, if you've had one or two large rate increases and your company's claims experience has been low or moderate, you are absolutely justified in asking your agent about finding you a new insurance company. As we mentioned in Chapter Three, there is a wide variation in rates for similar products in the same parts of the country among insurers.

Put pressure on your broker. Ask him or her the reason for the increase and whether all other businesses the insurer covers had the same rate increase. If this insurer has increased rates substantially for all businesses regardless of their claims experience, it may be time to look for another insurer. Sometimes insurers try to recoup previous losses by increasing rates, knowing that some groups will leave, but others won't go to the trouble of seeking a new carrier and will pay the price. Of course, your employees may have to go through the medical screening process ("underwriting," in insurance-ese) again if you do decide to switch. This means that employees' medical conditions which are covered by the current insurer might be excluded for a period of time by the new insurer.

Your broker should always understand that he or she risks losing your account to a different broker if you don't get good service. Remember, 5% to 10% of your premium helps pay his or her wages.

If, on the other hand, the reason for the rate hike is that your company has had a lot of claims, then one alternative is to seek out an insurer that doesn't charge a higher rate for poor health risks, possibly a Blue Cross/ Blue Shield plan.

If you discover that changing insurers won't lower your rates, try to save money by managing your costs or shifting some of them to your employees. As we discussed in Chapter Four, you can save money on your premiums by

1. Decreasing the benefit: increase deductible, increase coinsurance, lower the benefits.
2. Considering an HMO or PPO.
3. Moving from the HMO or PPO back to a traditional plan.
4. Seeing if a purchasing coalition has been set up in your area.
5. Increasing or initiating an employee contribution.

Q: Is it worth it to switch insurers?

Insurers are used to losing small business customers to another insurer with more competitive rates. It's not uncommon for one third of the small groups in an insurer's portfolio to leave for one reason or another in their first year.

A new insurer may be able to offer a lower price because the company is run more efficiently, or it expects to make a lower profit, or because it is trying to attract more customers with low prices—which will increase later.

The low price may also be the "teaser" rate in a durational pricing system, and you can expect rates to increase dramatically.

Another key reason why small businesses switch insurers is to get better service. Some insurers are simply better able to process claims than others.

Ironically, you could be making your broker happy if you switch insurers. The first-year commission for new business is often higher than the commission for renewal business!

QUESTIONS ABOUT COVERAGE

Q: *There's a lot of fine print. How can my employees tell if a certain procedure is covered by insurance?*

Most medical bills are for non-emergency treatment. Medical expenses such as childbirth, courses of physiotherapy and gallbladder removal can usually be planned in advance. So employees should be able to know what's covered and what isn't ahead of time. If the coverage isn't spelled out clearly enough in the policy or the employee handbook, the easiest way to find out what the insurer will pay is to call or write the insurer.

The employee should first ask the doctor and hospital ahead of time for the planned treatment (procedure code), the condition (diagnosis code) and how much the procedure will cost. Then call or write the insurer. Many insurers have toll-free numbers.

If it's an emergency procedure, the employee probably shouldn't be worrying about whether the insurer covers it or not anyway. Well-designed insurance policies should pay for all or most emergency treatments.

Q: *An employee submitted a claim and the insurer sent her back a form saying they won't pay. Now what?*

First check with the employee handbook or benefit description. Don't expect the insurer to cover something it explicitly says it won't.

If you've checked the rules and you think the employee deserves more, call your broker or the insurer. Insurers, like everyone else, make mistakes. If there's a legitimate reason why the insurer won't pay for coverage, it should be spelled out on the Explanation of Benefits (EOB) form, which is mailed to employees by the insurer whenever a claim is submitted. We've listed the typical reasons below, followed by an explanation of each.

1. Not a covered benefit or charge not allowed
2. Charge in excess of regular & customary—or—charge in excess of allowance: (results in partial payment)
3. Deductible
4. Coinsurance
5. Pre-certificiation/Second opinion not sought
6. Patient/dependent not covered
7. Insufficient documentation
8. Insurance premium not paid

9. Pre-existing condition
10. Benefit limits exceeded

"Not a covered benefit" is one of the most common reasons for non-payment. For example, most insurance policies will not pay for routine physical exams. Under a traditional Blue Cross/Blue Shield plan, non-hospital prescription drugs aren't covered. Other common examples: non-prescription drugs, such as most vitamins, and care rendered by a podiatrist or by a chiropractor. "Charge not allowed" is similar to "Not a covered benefit." Most plans exclude telephone charges or TV rental made during a hospital stay.

What to do about it: Check the employee handbook. Remember that claims processors make mistakes. The insurer could be confusing your company's coverage with someone else's. Also, make sure the original bill isn't in error.

"Charge in excess of xxxx," where xxxx can be something like, "regular and customary," "usual and customary," "usual, regular, and customary," or "allowance," or "eligible charge." The xxxx is how insurers limit what they will pay for any given procedure; it's the amount that the insurer will consider as a maximum.

What to do about it: The easiest way to follow up on this one is to ask the doctor's office why his or her fees are so unusually high. It's probably easier to convince the doctor that he or she should lower fees than to fight the insurer on this one.

"Deductible" This is an amount you have to pay under certain contracts. If there is a deductible, the insurer will pay nothing until you pay medical bills up to the amount of the deductible. For example, if your benefits specify a $200 deductible per year, then the first $200 of *eligible* doctor or hospital bills is paid by the insured person, not the insurer.

One key is "eligible." If the plan doesn't cover faith healers or acupuncture, nothing you spend on them counts toward the deductible.

What to do about it: Deductibles can be complicated. Check your benefits for deductible "loopholes." For example, it's possible that you didn't "use up" your deductible last year and you may be able to apply part of last year's expenses to this year's deductible. Also, some policies don't require you to pay a deductible in the event the injury was caused by an accident.

"Coinsurance" is a percent of the eligible bill that you have to pay. Most of the time it's 80% or 90%. Sometimes you have to pay coinsurance if you don't get a second opinion on non-emergency surgery; for example, if you get the second opinion the insurer might pay 100% for the treatment; otherwise it might only pay 80%.

What to do about it: If co-insurance is required for certain procedures, you've got to cough up the rest of the bill. Most policies contain "out-of-pocket" maximums after which the coinsurance is 100%. Check the policy for this feature.

"Second opinion/pre-certification not sought" Many policies *require* you to get insurer approval or two doctors to check you over before the insurer will pay for certain operations. As we pointed out in Chapter Four, pre-certification and second opinion requirements are a cost-containment measure insurers take to make sure they don't waste money on unnecessary procedures.

What to do about it: If you didn't follow the rules, there isn't much you can do. But you may have an "out" if the treatment was a genuine emergency; mandatory second opinion programs usually make exceptions for emergency operations. Contact your insurer.

"Patient/dependent not covered" This means that when the people in the claims processing department looked up the patient's name to see if he or she was eligible for coverage, they couldn't find the name. The insurance company thinks the employee or dependent isn't covered by the insurance.

What to do about it: If the patient is supposed to be covered, protest. This error could happen if the employee didn't fill in the proper forms to enroll himself or herself or the kids. Employees should alert you whenever there's a new dependent (or spouse).

"Insufficient Documentation" Most insurers require a detailed claim form to be filled out before they will pay. The employee probably forgot to fill in a blank somewhere.

What to do about it: The simplest thing to do is to read the EOB form or to call the insurer and find out what's missing. If you pay your bills and submit them for reimbursement, make sure your bills include at least the following:

1. Patient's name.
2. Doctor's (or other provider's) name and address.
3. Doctor's (or other provider's) Tax Identification Number (TIN), a nine-digit number like a social security number.
4. The diagnosis (usually a Latin name and a multi-digit "ICD code")—this is the condition or symptom.
5. The procedure (again a Latin name and a multi-digit "CPT code")—this is what the doctor did to fix the condition or symptom.
6. The date of service.
7. The charge.
8. Receipts—be sure to keep copies of everything you send the insurer.

"Insurance premium not paid" Just as it sounds: You forgot to pay your premium—or you did pay it and it got lost.

What to do about it: Be ready to resubmit the bill. The insurer may have screwed up. But even if the premium was not paid there are some "safety nets." You may have a grace period, as we mentioned earlier in the chapter.

"Pre-existing condition" Insurers don't want to sell insurance to someone who is already sick. If you've got a heart condition, you may be considered "uninsurable."

What to do about it: You can try to prove to the insurer that the condition treated doesn't fit into their definition of preexisting conditions. For example, you may have had a bad knee for years, but it hasn't bothered you for the last year. In this case, if the definition of a preexisting condition is something for which you've had treatment or symptoms in the past six months, then your claim isn't "preexisting." Read the conditions carefully. A note from your doctor may help.

"Benefit limits exceeded" Most policies have several limits. There is usually an overall limit on how much the insurer will pay on an employee's behalf in his or her lifetime, ranging from $250,000 to $1,000,000. Sometimes these limits are for families instead of individuals. There are also often separate, lower "inside limits" on services such as mental and nervous conditions.

What to do about it: Most limits are annual limits. For these kinds of limits, the new calendar year will wipe the slate clean. The big limits (like $1,000,000) are usually lifetime limits, but they often contain a clause that restores several thousand dollars of benefits each year after the limit has been met. If you have what's called a base plus supplementary major medical plan—typically a no-frills Blues base plan combined with a commercial plan that supplements the base plan—expenses that are beyond the limits in the base may be reimbursed under the major medical part of the program. As a last resort, the employee may have to turn to Medicare or Medicaid for help.

CHAPTER 6
WELLNESS PROGRAMS: THE APPLE-A-DAY APPROACH

Small business owners may rule out the wellness phenomenon as a fad whose time will come and go, like hula hoops and bell bottoms. But don't equate the notion of healthy living with gravity shoes, oat bran or other short-lived preoccupations of the health nut set.

Wellness can mean educating employees that if they simply change their health habits by chucking cigarettes or cutting out the wrong kind of cholesterol, they can live longer and feel better. And that means lower health costs for you either immediately or in the long run. Your employees' scores on the "Healthstyle" quiz (Figure 6-1) may help you decide whether to implement a wellness program in your own company.

HEALTH PROMOTION PROGRAMS

While we couldn't find any comparable data on smaller firms, two of three firms with 50 employees or more now offer some health-promotion activity, says a 1989 study in the *American Journal of Public Health*. Health promotion programs range from distributing pamphlets on health issues to providing showers or changing facilities for employees who exercise.

One type of health promotion program, health risk screening, directly relates to health care by providing testing for high blood pressure, breast cancer, diabetes and high cholesterol levels.

Figure 6-1

HEALTHSTYLE

A Self-Test

	Almost Always	Sometimes	Almost Never
CIGARETTE SMOKING			
If you *never smoke*, enter a score of 10 for this section and go to the next section on *Alcohol and Drugs*.			
1. I avoid smoking cigarettes.	2	1	0
2. I smoke only low tar and nicotine cigarettes *or* I smoke a pipe or cigars.	2	1	0
Smoking Score: _____			
ALCOHOL AND DRUGS			
1. I avoid drinking alcoholic beverages *or* I drink no more than 1 or 2 drinks a day.	4	1	0

2. I avoid using alcohol or other drugs (especially illegal drugs) as a way of handling stressful situations or the problems in my life.   2   1   0

3. I am careful not to drink alcohol when taking certain medicines (for example, medicine for sleeping, pain, colds, and allergies), or when pregnant.   2   1   0

4. I read and follow the label directions when using prescribed and over-the-counter drugs.   2   1   0

Alcohol and Drugs Score: _____

EATING HABITS

1. I eat a variety of foods each day, such as fruits and vegetables, whole grain breads, and cereals, lean meats, dairy products, dry peas and beans, and nuts and seeds.   4   1   0

2. I limit the amount of fat, saturated fat, and cholesterol I eat (including fat on meats, eggs, butter, cream, shortenings, and organ meats such as liver).   2   1   0

3. I limit the amount of salt I eat by cooking with only small amounts, not adding salt at the table, and avoiding salty snacks.   2   1   0

4. I avoid eating too much sugar (especially frequent snacks of sticky candy or soft drinks).   2   1   0

Eating Habits Score: _____

EXERCISE/FITNESS

1. I maintain a desired weight, avoiding overweight and underweight.   3   1   0

2. I do vigorous exercises for 15-30 minutes at least 3 times a week (examples include running, swimming, brisk walking).   3   1   0

3. I do exercises that enhance my muscle tone for 15-30 minutes at least 3 times a week (examples include yoga and calisthenics).   2   1   0

4. I use part of my leisure time participating in individual, family, or team activities that increase my level of fitness (such as gardening, bowling, golf, and baseball).   2   1   0

Exercise/Fitness Score: _____

STRESS CONTROL

1. I have a job or do other work that I enjoy.   2   1   0

2. I find it easy to relax and express my feelings freely.   2   1   0

3. I recognize early, and prepare for, events or situations likely to be stressful for me.   2   1   0

4. I have close friends, relatives, or others whom I can talk to about personal matters and call on for help when needed.   2   1   0

5. I participate in group activities (such as church and community organizations) or hobbies that I enjoy.   2   1   0

Stress Control Score: _____

	Almost Always	Sometimes	Almost Never
SAFETY			
1. I wear a seat belt while riding in a car.	2	1	0
2. I avoid driving while under the influence of alcohol and other drugs.	2	1	0
3. I obey traffic rules and the speed limit when driving.	2	1	0
4. I am careful when using potentially harmful products or substances (such as household cleaners, poisons, and electrical devices).	2	1	0
5. I avoid smoking in bed.	2	1	0

Safety Score: _____

What Your Scores On Each Section Mean to YOU

SCORES OF 9 AND 10
Excellent! Your answers show that you are aware of the importance of this area to your health. More important, you are putting your knowledge to work for you by practicing good health habits. As long as you continue to do so, this area should not pose a serious health risk. It's likely that you are setting an example for your family and friends to follow. Since you got a very high test score on this part of the test, you may want to consider other areas where your scores indicate room for improvement.

SCORES OF 6 TO 8
Your health practices in this area are good, but there is room for improvement. Look again at the items you answered with a "Sometimes" or "Almost Never." What changes can you make to improve your score? Even a small change can often help you achieve better health.

SCORES OF 3 TO 5
Your health risks are showing! Would you like more information about the risks you are facing and about why it is important for you to change these behaviors. Perhaps you need help in deciding how to successfully make the changes you desire. In either case, help is available.

SCORES OF 0 TO 2
Obviously, you were concerned enough about your health to take the test, but your answers show that you may be taking serious and unnecessary risks with your health. Perhaps you are not aware of the risks and what to do about them. You can easily get the information and help you need to improve, if you wish. The next step is up to you.

SOURCE: *Wellness at the Worksite*, by Health Insurance Assoc. of America and American Council of Life Insurance.

Other programs involve classes and seminars on such topics as good nutrition and ways to stop smoking, lose weight, and manage stress.

There is little doubt that there is a direct relationship between getting somebody to stop smoking and lowering their risk of getting lung cancer. Smoking is the leading avoidable cause of death and disease and the biggest culprit in heart disease and cancer.

Two cigarettes a day doubles your risk of contracting lung cancer, three triples it, and so on up to 20. According to some studies, two years after you stop smoking your chance of having a heart attack returns to normal and ten years later the added risk of lung cancer virtually disappears.

Neither is there much doubt that employees who smoke cost companies more. Health claims of employees who smoke are on average $285 higher than those who don't, according to a recent study of one large company by Travelers Insurance Co. and the University of Michigan.

Some employers pay a portion of the cost for employees to attend clinics to stop smoking or pay a higher percentage of medical insurance premiums for employees who do not smoke or who regularly participate in an exercise program. Others set up competitions among employees with prizes awarded to winners, or offer bonuses to employees who complete a specified number of hours of exercise. Companies with health promotion programs generally report lower absenteeism rates, lower health care costs, and more productive employees. Some larger companies evaluate their programs by comparing the fitness of exercise program participants with that of a control group, measuring such factors as weight control, smoking cessation, elevated blood pressure, and the number of sick days used.

But do wellness programs work? Employees in fitness programs have lower turnover rates, lower absenteeism (one to four fewer sick days a year), lower health care costs (saving $100 to $1,000 per year per employee), and fewer hospital and rehabilitation days after injury, according to a study published in *Business Insurance* in 1990.

On the other hand, others say the jury's not in. Some critics of wellness programs cite "adverse selection" as one of the reasons why they're not effective. In other words, the younger, healthier employees are the ones who are usually likely to join exercise programs—not the older couch potatoes who would most benefit.

On the other hand, very few dispute the fact that the converse is true: that employees who engage in "unwellness" (i.e., who smoke and have heart disease) cost companies more.

In a landmark study of its health care claims from 1980 to 1982, Control Data Corp. found that high-risk employees—those who smoked, had high blood pressure, were overweight or rarely exercised—cost the company hundreds of dollars more each year in medical claims than their low-risk colleagues. For example, employees who smoke at least one pack of cigarettes a day generate 18% higher health care claims than non-smokers. People at high risk for hypertension have 11% higher health claims. People who are more than 30% overweight have health claims that are 11% higher than those who are 20% overweight.

Ask your insurer if you can save on your premiums by having healthy employees. Travelers Insurance offers discounts of up to 12% for companies of ten to 49 employees if they rate favorably on several risk factors. John Alden Life Insurance Co. in Miami offers similar discounts for companies of 25 or fewer employees in the Southeast.

Wellness programs need not strip the treasury bare. Many companies take advantage of free or low-cost screenings and workshops offered by community outreach programs at local hospitals and by nonprofit health organizations such as the American Heart Association, the National Cancer Society, and the March of Dimes. A fitness program need involve no more than the cost of a VCR and a few tapes or the purchase of T-shirts for employee sports teams.

Here are some examples of companies that have successful wellness programs. While not all the companies mentioned are small, all of the programs are sufficiently low-cost that they could be undertaken by a small company.

Overall Fitness

Smoking and excess pounds are the most common targets of wellness programs, but some companies extend their programs to such risk factors as blood pressure, cholesterol levels, use of car seat belts and other healthy, life-prolonging habits.

Scherer Brothers, a Minneapolis lumber company with 280 employees, took a "you are what you put in your mouth" approach to wellness. It removed all cigarette and candy machines from the premises, replaced regular coffee with decaffeinated, and offers free healthful lunches and snacks to employees.

Employees are offered classes and educational materials on quitting smoking, losing weight, and preventing back injuries. They can have their blood pressure monitored if they wish and may take part in the company's yearly cancer screenings. Scherer Brothers also gives bonuses to those who were not absent or late during specified periods.

As a result, absenteeism at the company is about one-eighth the industry average.

Southern California Edison offers a five-point screening program that checks not only smoking and weight but blood sugar, blood pressure, and cholesterol. Employees who pass the voluntary test or who can obtain a doctor's certificate that they are in a program to improve any deficiencies get $10 a month from the company. That $120 a year is enough to offset the employee's required contribution to the company's medical program.

In 1988, the utility's costs dropped to $82 million from $100 million the year before. It expected its 1989-1990 costs to rise as little as 14% instead of the usual 23%.

At *Provident Indemnity Life Insurance Co.* in Norristown, Pennsylvania, employees get a bonus if they don't use their sick pay. All employees get a health risk appraisal and personalized feedback. No smoking is allowed anywhere; smokers pay a higher life insurance premium. Monthly educational programs cover stress, nutrition, hearing testing, high blood pressure screening, etc. A walking club meets at lunchtime. By wearing seat belts, learning CPR, and attending monthly educational programs, employees can win points toward prizes such as a sweat suit or gym bag. A weight loss program is conducted by the local dairy council.

First Interstate Bank of Santa Fe, New Mexico arranges discounts for health club memberships. Every Wednesday morning fruit is available free—resulting in a 75% reduction in doughnut consumption during those periods. Employees and their families can take advantage of six visits to a counseling service for personal problems such as marital difficulties, emotional problems, or drug/alcohol conditions.

Bodolay-Pratt of Lakeland, Florida, provides high blood pressure and glaucoma screening through the local hospital. The company also removed cigarette machines from the premises.

Quaker Oats Co. offers workers tips on keeping fit, tips on cutting medical costs, and cash bonuses to employees who stay healthy. Kathy Kahn is one of 10,000 employees who received bonuses averaging $150 in 1987 as a reward for helping keep the company's rise in health costs to just over 5%. "With this plan I feel I have a certain amount of control over my health benefits," says Ms. Kahn.

Each year Quaker budgets a medical "expense account" for each worker. If an employee doesn't use his full allotment, he gets a refund.

Smoking Cessation, Weight Control

The price of tobacco for some 37,000 workers at *Baker Hughes Inc.* is higher than for other folks: any tobacco user at the Houston-based firm now has to pay $10 a month more for health insurance.

At *U-Haul International* employees and spouses who are overweight and who smoke pay $10 a month more for health insurance.

Pointe Resorts, operator of three large resort hotels in Phoenix, pays 90% of the health insurance premium for executives who don't smoke and are the proper weight for their size. For smokers and the obese, the company will pay only half.

Cancer Screening

Cancer affects one in five Americans and the medical treatment for just one late-detected cancer can cost $60,000 or more, estimates the American Cancer Society. In 1985 *Pennzoil Co.* began a cancer screening program. Some 4,900 employees participated at a cost of $20 a person.

Pre-cancerous conditions were detected and treated in 150 employees, including two top executives. Fourteen malignant conditions were diagnosed and treated. "If even two of those individuals had not been screened and treated, the costs to the company would easily have exceeded that $100,000 investment," says Richard Howe, retired president and COO of Pennzoil.

Seatbelt Use

Carol Biederman never bothered to buckle up when she would drive 30 minutes each day to work as a secretary at the office of a Boston-area health consulting firm. Then her employer, *Hewitt Associates*, offered her and its other employees $50 if they pledged to wear their seat belts. She did, and a month later an 18-wheel truck crashed into her car on the Massachusetts Turnpike. She emerged unscathed.

"Now I would never drive down the street without buckling up completely," said Biederman.

At Hewitt, employees also get $50 for not smoking and $50 for submitting to a battery of screenings: cholesterol, blood pressure, urine, blood sugar, and weight. They can opt for cash or a rebate in health premiums.

Exercise

At *Safeway Bakery* in Clackamas, Oregon, employees built a fitness center on their own time, and now manage the facility and pay dues to cover expenses. The center is open to employees, families, and friends 24 hours a day. Points are gained through regular fitness evaluations; employees earn T-shirts containing the company's wellness theme, "Buns on the Run."

Maupintour Inc., a vacation tour company with 165 employees, built a small fitness center at its headquarters in Lawrence, Kansas, in 1981, outfitting it with a treadmill, stationary bikes, weights, sauna, and lockers. The company hires only nonsmokers, bans smoking in its offices, and sponsors sports teams. Employees who meet monthly fitness goals set by themselves and a fitness expert get T-shirts, shorts, warm-up jackets, etc.

While it's not clear how much of its $5,000 investment has been paid back in fewer lost work days or medical costs, Maupintour's personnel director John Gibson says, "Our insurance rates haven't gone up like other companies in the area."

At *Stevens Real Estate*, Lawrence, Kansas, mini-trampolines are used by employees, including sales people, while listening to sales training tapes.

Probably the granddaddy of all the corporate wellness programs is *Johnson & Johnson*'s "Live for Life" program, which it not only offers to its 30,000-person work force, but also has marketed to other corporations. One client is Saatchi & Saatchi, the advertising giant. Johnson & Johnson built an on-site health club at Saatchi & Saatchi's New York headquarters. Employees pay between $10 and $20 monthly for aerobics classes, exercise machines, and health seminars.

You don't have to have a gym to hold exercise classes, the gym can come to you. Fitness Plus Inc. in New York City runs classes in makeshift exercise rooms: a conference room, a dining area. Employers or employees can pay the tab (about $5 each a session).

RECOMMENDATIONS

1. Contact the American Heart Association and American Cancer Association for information about screening.
2. Offer smokers a bonus to quit. Make it a worthwhile sum—like two to five times their daily wages. Consider making your worksite smoke-free.
3. Be careful about encouraging employee involvement in sports. A little too much exercise can be a dangerous thing if someone is injured or overextended. The cost of sports injuries can exceed the cost benefits of exercise.
4. Make sure your snack machines include fruit and fruit juices.
5. Tell your insurance agent what you're doing. He or she may be able to get a better rate for you or find you a different insurer that gives discounts for wellness.

FOR MORE INFORMATION

Publications

Wellness in Small Business, Washington Business Group on Health, 1985, 14 pages, $15. One of a series of wellness pamphlets produced by this organization. The series is $230. Call (202) 408-9320 or write 777 North Capitol Street NE, Suite 800, Washington, D.C. 20002.

Employee Health Promotion: A Guide for Starting Programs at the Workplace, HealthWorks Northwest, 1983, 92 pages, $15. Step-by-step instructions liberally sprinkled with examples. Identifies key decision points where "go, no-go" decisions must be made. Write to Puget Sound Health Systems Agency, 601 Valley St., Seattle, WA 98109.

A Practical Planning Guide for Employee Health Promotion Programs, Health Planning Council Inc., 1982, 45 pages, $4.00. This publication provides a step-by-step approach to developing health promotion programs, highlighting benefits, evaluation, legal and financial risk considerations, and some dos and don'ts. Write 995 Applegate Road, Madison, WI 53713.

Work to be Well: A Small Business Guide to Wellness at the Workplace, Health Systems Agency of Western Lake Superior, 1982, 115 pages, $5. Contains strategies for planning programs, including those that businesses can do on their own. Write Health Projects Office, Health Systems Agency of Western Lake Superior, 202 Ordean Building, 424 West Superior St., Duluth, MN 55802.

Your Guide to Wellness at the Worksite, Health Insurance Association of America, 1983, 18 pages, 60 cents. Describes actual programs being undertaken. Special focus on smoking cessation. Lists voluntary organizations and government agencies that can help out. Write 1001 Pennsylvania Avenue NW, Washington, D.C. 20004-2599.

Helping Your Employees to Protect Themselves Against Cancer, American Cancer Society, 1981, 48 pages, single copy free. How to provide education on four major cancers: colorectal, lung, breast, and uterine. Write your local ACS chapter.

Cardiovascular Primer for the Workplace, Department of Health and Human Services, 1981, 88 pages, single copy free. Describes what factors to consider when adopting a health promotion program targeting cardiovascular disease. Write High Blood Pressure Information Center, 120/80 National Institutes of Health, Box WS, Bethesda, MD 20205.

Blood Pressure Control at the Worksite: Manual of Procedures for Blood Pressure Control Programs in Industrial Settings, Institute of Labor and Industrial Relations, 1979, 83 pages, $5. Procedures for setting up a blood pressure control program. Details follow-up, record keeping and program evaluation. Write The Worker Health Program, 401 Fourth St., Ann Arbor, MI 48103.

Organizations

The Center for Corporate Health Promotion, 1850 Centennial Park Drive, Suite 520, Reston, VA 22091; (703) 391-1921. Offers products and support for lifestyle-management programs.

Washington Business Group on Health, 2291/2 Pennsylvania Avenue SE, Washington, D.C. 20003; (202) 547-6644. The group's prevention leadership forum publishes reports on worksite wellness subjects. The reports are $15 each or $210 for the full set of 16. We highly recommend one of the pamphlets, *Wellness in Small Business,* (discussed above) for its anecdotes about success stories in various small companies.

Association for Fitness in Business, 310 North Alabama St., Suite A100, Indianapolis, IN 46204; (317) 636-6621. Can supply names of businesses and consultants in your area to help you start a wellness program.

National Health Information Clearinghouse, P.O. Box 1133, Washington, D.C. 20013; (202) 565-4167. Offers information and referral services for 1,000 health related agencies and will supply you free lifestyle check-up form to help employees appraise their personal health.

CHAPTER 7
BUYING DISABILITY INSURANCE

Disability income benefits compensate a worker who can't work because of an illness or injury—which can be anyone from somebody who broke his back in a car accident to an individual infected with the HIV virus to a woman who recently gave birth. Disabling conditions can include arthritis, heart attacks, strokes and diabetes.

There are a number of reasons to provide disability coverage to your employees. For one thing, it's much more likely that an employee will become disabled for 90 days or more before reaching age 65 than he or she will die. Chances are one in three that an employee will have a work-stopping health problem lasting at least one month before he or she reaches age 65, according to *Fundamentals of Employee Benefits*, by the Employee Benefit Research Institute. By the year 2000, disability benefits may cost business and government as much as $200 billion a year.

The other reason to provide the coverage is because your employees are much less likely to buy disability insurance on their own than they are to buy life insurance. And without disability coverage, a disabled employee would have to rely exclusively on social security benefits—benefits that are only awarded in the case of a severe disability.

Even when employees do qualify for them, social security benefits are pretty skimpy compared to most professionals' incomes. The average benefit that somebody earning at least $51,000 a year or $4,250 a month can get is about $1,100 a month or $1,700 for a family, versus the $2,550 he'd get from a disability policy that pays 60% of income.

Unlike pension plans, a company can choose special disability benefits for executives whether or not the company has a regular long-term disability program for all of its employees or if the regular program provides limited benefits. The employer is free to choose who will be covered, the amount of coverage, and the terms of the coverage.

In Chapter Three we described occupations that are considered to be high-risk by insurers, meaning that the people in these jobs can have a tough time finding coverage or pay more for it. Well, there's good news: The people who sell you disability insurance have also outlined industries they think are low risks. Interestingly enough, they're some of the same occupations considered high medical care risks!

Here are lower risk industries

- Banking
- Savings and loan associations
- Ad agencies
- Computer and data processing companies

- Research and development companies
- Management consultants and public relations companies
- Health professionals
- Legal services
- Education (as long as you're in the suburbs or the country)
- Engineering and architectural services
- Accounting, auditing, and bookkeeping

Both short-term and long-term disability plans are usually defined as the employee's inability to perform his or her job as a result of a sickness or accident, as certified by a physician. Benefits usually aren't payable if the employee isn't under a physician's care or if the injury is self-inflicted. Under the 1978 pregnancy amendment to Title VII of the Civil Rights Act of 1964, companies must provide coverage for disabilities resulting from pregnancy on the same basis as disabilities arising from other causes. (Don't confuse this with maternity benefits.)

The trick in designing a disability program is to adequately compensate employees while they're not collecting a salary but not be so generous as to encourage employees to "extend" the period of disability (otherwise known as malingering.)

Long-term disability plans are those that provide benefits for two years or more. They are usually designed to provide income to employees who are unable to return to work. Short-term disability plans tend to have a higher claim frequency but aren't as expensive.

Not all companies approach the disability issue in the same way. Some companies have no formal plan at all; some only offer short-term coverage, some only long term.

Sick Pay

Many businesses have an informal short-term plan especially for professional staff in which salary is continued during brief periods of illness before even short-term disability kicks in. This is called sick pay. Under some schemes, the duration of sick leave benefits depends on length of service with the employer. Sick leave usually provides 100% of a worker's normal earnings.

Short-Term Plans

Group short-term plans may also be referred to as sickness and accident benefits, non-occupational sickness and accident disability benefits, accident and sickness plans, etc. They may be either insured or self-insured. For large employers, short-term sicknesses are fairly predictable and self-insurance is common.

The amount of weekly income benefits in short-term plans is usually related to earnings and ranges from 50% to 67% of earnings. If you get more generous than that, employees may "malinger."

Short-term plans typically have a maximum benefit duration of 13, 26, or 52 weeks, with a waiting period of a few days. Some plans waive the waiting period in the case of an accident-caused disability under the theory that plans without waiting periods will invite abuse, but few employees will deliberately have an accident in order to collect benefits.

Because short-term disability covers the period before long-term disability, the amounts of individual claims won't ever be very high. For example, if the short-term benefit starts after an employee has been sick for one week and stops after six months, the maximum benefit for one period of sickness will be 25 weeks.

While this may seem like a big risk for an employer, it's very much less than the maximum length of benefits for long-term disability, which could last for over 40 years. That's why long-term disability is insured more often than short-term.

Very small groups—fewer than ten employees—may have trouble buying short-term disability coverage. As with health insurance, there is a high risk to the insurer that the owner himself (or other key employee) may have bought the policy deliberately to cover an expensive condition.

Five states require companies to offer short-term disability benefits along with Puerto Rico: Rhode Island, California, New Jersey, New York, and Hawaii. These laws are designed to provide some cash disability benefits for non-work-connected temporary disabilities. The benefits, related to a worker's earnings, are payable after a short waiting period, such as one week.

LONG-TERM PLANS

Long-term benefits are considered to be those lasting two years or more, but they usually have a duration of at least five years, depending on the employee's length of service. The vast majority of plans have a benefit period up to a limiting age, such as 65 or 70.

Long-term disability plans have waiting periods before the benefit payments begin during which the insured person must be under the care of a physician and not working. Waiting periods can range from three to 12 months or more.

Long-term disability plans normally have a stricter definition of disability than short-term plans. The traditional approach is a two-phase one. In the first phase the employee must be completely unable to work in his or her occupation for a specified period of time, such as two to five years. Then, after this period, the disabled employee can keep getting payments only if he or she is completely unable to engage in *any* gainful occupation.

One obvious problem with the traditional approach is that the "any occupation" clause could force a brain surgeon to sort mail when he'd most likely want to work in his own profession.

A relatively recent insurance product which aims to help professionals get back to work is called the partial disability benefit. This benefit allows an employee to return to work part time in his or her own occupation or another occupation after being totally disabled for a short period of time, but deducts something like 50% of his or her earnings from the disability benefits. The theory behind this design is to reward the employee who can return to work and thereby encourage rehabilitation. Rehabilitation benefits are also included.

According to the Employee Benefit Research Institute, rehabilitation programs such as these can save employers and insurers big money, as well as help the individual regain a productive life.

A problem with the partial disability benefit is that benefits start only after the insured meets the definition of total disability for a certain period. This may have the effect of encouraging the disability lifestyle and malingering. As a result, the "zero-day residual" was introduced, meaning that partial disability payments will be made even if the insured hasn't met the total disability requirements at all.

A fourth kind of insurance benefit is known as income replacement coverage. The policies don't test the insured person's ability to perform on the job, but require a 20% or more reduction in earnings due to the disability if, for example, the person could only work part-time.

Disability plans are typically available only to regular full-time employees. Unlike medical expense plans, disability income plans usually have a long probationary period of employment before employees become eligible to participate. It's not unusual for the probationary period to be one year of service.

As with health coverage, many long-term disability plans covering small companies (fewer than 100 employees) limit coverage for preexisting conditions. A typical provision might say that benefits aren't payable for a disability that begins within one year after the insurance goes into effect, if the cause of the disability began within three months before the employee became insured.

Benefits can range from 50% to 70% of salary, although some plans provide benefits as high as 75% to 80% of earnings. Again, insurers are concerned that over-generous benefits would encourage employees to malinger.

As with short-term benefits, certain injuries are excluded: those that are self-inflicted, those due to war or those that arise while committing a crime. Also, long-term disability plans may exclude or limit benefits for mental disorders, alcoholism, and drug addiction.

Some long-term disability benefits offer a cost-of-living increase option, meaning that the benefit increases with inflation.

Survivor benefits are available that pay lump sum multiples of the monthly disability benefit if the employee dies while disabled. This may duplicate coverage under life insurance benefits, provided the life insurance coverage continues while the employee is disabled.

Some insurers also offer optional education benefits to help pay for the tuition of dependents of disabled employees.

Integrating Disability Payments With Other Benefits

As with short-term disability benefits, long-term disability payments should be integrated or coordinated with payments from workers' compensation insurance, social security or similar programs.

In relating the level of benefits to an employee's income, keep in mind that many people receiving long-term disability may also be entitled to social security benefits, which are partially income tax-free. For that reason, long term disability plans are almost always integrated or coordinated with other types of disability benefits that the employee might be entitled to. For example, a benefit plan might stipulate that the total combined monthly benefits from the employer and government can't exceed a certain percentage of monthly salary.

There are several ways of integrating these payments, including:

1. Reducing benefits by the amounts the employee or the employee plus his family receives from governmental or other employer disability plan.
2. Reducing benefits to no more than 70% of the previous salary.

The advantage of an offset to the insurer is obvious: costs are reduced. The disadvantage to the employee is moderated by the fact that the offset is fixed at the time the benefit is calculated. The offset doesn't increase as social security benefits increase, so some degree of inflation protection is provided.

Regulations and Taxes

Under the 1986 amendments to the Age Discrimination in Employment Act (ADEA), plans that provide disability benefits must not have an upper age limit on active employees' eligibility for these benefits. Companies with at least 20 employees working for at least 20 weeks a year must comply with this law.

Employers usually meet the ADEA requirements by spending the same amount of premium dollars on older employees as they do on younger ones. Since premiums for disability insurance increase with age, the net result would be that the older employee gets a reduced benefit: either the same benefit for a shorter duration or lower benefit.

Tax status: Employers can deduct their contribution to premium payments but employees can't. Benefits are usually taxable to the employee if the employer pays the premium but not if the employee pays the premium.

This means that an employee-pay-all disability program actually would give the employee tax-free disability income, which can be a considerable increase over the benefits available from a seemingly equivalent employer-paid program. One problem with an employee-paid program is that insurers will require a high percentage of the employees of small companies to participate or won't offer the insurance. Insurers are concerned that if a majority of people don't participate, the ones who do will tend to be people who expect to be disabled.

Participation requirements are usually 100% if the employer pays all or 75% if the employee pays. For groups of fewer than 10, insurers may require 100% no matter who pays.

Disability coverage typically terminates on the same day that an employee leaves the company, or within a short period such as a month. There is usually no continuation of disability coverage during layoffs or during leaves of absence. Also, unlike group life insurance and medical expense benefits, there is no state- or federally-mandated option for continuation of disability benefits after an employee leaves the company, but some insurers offer the option. Like some life insurance policies, policies insurers waive the collection of premiums for an individual who is disabled.

WHAT YOU'LL PAY

Here are some sample rates for a very small employer policy that offers a 90-day waiting period before the benefits kick in, pays 60% of salary up to age 65, and defines disability as the inability to perform one's own occupation (as opposed to doing any old job).

Age	Annual rate per $100 of salary
Under 35	$ 0.45
35-40	0.65
41-45	1.00
46-50	1.65
51-55	2.50
55-60	3.11
61-64	3.20

Here's how this works out annually: an employer would pay $325 a year to cover a 39-year-old earning $50,000 a year.

Remember, these rates will vary depending on the insurer and whether your company is in a high risk industry or occupation. But as with health insurance, there are opportunities to lower your rates. You can do so by increasing the waiting period before benefits begin to 180 days and by agreeing to define disability as the inability to perform *any* occupation after two years. (For the first two years the definition would still be considered the person's own occupation.) Your rates will also probably go down as the size of the company increases—don't forget to tell your agent when you add a significant number of employees.

DISABILITY COVERAGE THAT'S REALLY BUSINESS PROTECTION INSURANCE

There are small company disability policies that aren't really employee benefits, they're employer benefits—they keep the company running if something happens to the "brains" of it, i.e., you or your partner.

When disability strikes the owner or another key person in a small business, there are two problems. First, there is the need to continue the employee/owner's income without unduly burdening the company. Secondly, if it doesn't look like the disabled person is going to recover, he or she will want to sell his or her interest to someone else. So this benefit gives money to the co-owners who aren't disabled to buy the other owner out.

Business Protection for Small Businesses

Disability income: Monthly benefits are paid directly to the disabled owner who decides how that money is spent. Disability income coverage helps a business owner meet personal obligations, such as a home mortgage, utilities, food bills and auto payments, as well as business obligations at a time when the business probably isn't generating much income.

Benefits begin anywhere from 30 days to one year after the onset of a disability and can last from two years to as long as the individual lives. The generosity built into some plans also affects the cost of the policy; the sooner benefits are payable and the longer they last, the more expensive the policy.

As a small business owner, you can also buy a residual disability rider that permits you to collect benefits if you are partially disabled, i.e., you can still work in your occupation but the disability causes you to lose revenues. Usually, in order to qualify for the benefit, your disability has to prevent you from performing one or more of your important daily duties or from performing them for as much time as usual, and you have to have lost at least 20% of your gross monthly revenue as a result of the disability.

Key employee disability insurance: This plan provides a monthly payment to help reimburse the business for the loss of services of a valuable employee other than the business owner. The payments can be used to replace income or lost profits.

Overhead expense disability insurance: If the owner becomes totally disabled, this insurance pays customary business expenses such as rent, electricity, telephone, heat, water, janitorial or maintenance services, taxes, and mortgage payments. This may or may not include employees' salaries.

Your benefit is calculated by subtracting your current gross monthly revenue from your disability benefit. You can also buy riders each year that cover any additional overhead expense until you reach age 55.

Insurance companies may also offer a professional overhead expense policy for sole proprietors which pays their expenses if they become totally disabled. If a professional replacement is hired to perform a sole proprietor's duties, 80% of his or her salary will be considered a covered overhead expense for up to six months.

Benefits usually begin 30, 60, or 90 days after a disability and are payable until the maximum benefit amount has been reached. Although the benefits are taxed as business income, the premiums for the policy are tax deductible.

Disability buyout insurance provides the funds needed to buy out the business interest of a totally disabled co-owner. One such company that offers this product provides income for a disabled stockholder/employee during the first year of disability, with benefits starting after a 30-day waiting period. The second phase of coverage deals with the prolonged disability that lasts longer than a year, at which point the buyout takes place. Most buyout agreements take one of three approaches:

1. A wait-and-see approach: In this scenario, disability buyout coverage isn't involved because the disabled person dies and his life insurance payout (with the co-owners as beneficiaries) provides the capital to buy out his interest in the business.

2. Readjustment of ownership rights: a disabled owner's stake in the business is traded for a limited partnership or preferred nonvoting stock. This assures the disabled owner of a fixed return on investment and relieves the firm of a potentially dissident voice in management.

3. Mandatory purchase: The firm or the other owners purchase the entire interest of the disabled associate for a price agreed upon in advance. Ownership is transferred at once, the money being paid either in a lump sum or in installments. This agreement might also make provisions for the associate's possible recovery, in which event the disabled person would have the option of buying back his or her own interest in the business.

Recommendations on Business Protection Coverage

You should get expert legal and accounting advice before investing in disability insurance that provides business protection policies. The regulations and tax implications of the various kinds of coverage are complicated and depend partly upon how the ownership of the company is structured. Key tax questions are: whether the premiums are deductible to the company, whether the premiums are considered income to covered employees, and whether the benefits are taxable to the recipient.

CHAPTER 8
BUYING WORKERS' COMPENSATION INSURANCE

When factory worker Jose C. complained of stomach pains, his boss, Steven K., sent him to a doctor, who said that cutting out coffee and spicy food would do the trick. But Jose C. blamed the ailment on stress and filed a workers' compensation claim for $1,900 for medical exams. Under California law, Steven K.'s company is liable for such expenses even though Jose C. dropped the claim when his condition improved.

The cost of premiums for workers' compensation insurance, which compensates employees for lost wages and medical bills as a result of a work-related ailment, have tripled at Steven K.'s company in the past ten years. Based on an increased number of claims, Steven K. fears his company's premiums could double to about $140,000—more than one-third of his expected profits of $400,000.

The cost of providing workers' compensation, independently regulated by each state, "is one of the top concerns in surveys of our members," says a spokesman for the National Federation of Independent Businesses, a trade group representing some 576,000 small businesses.

Let's state from the outset that small employers probably have even less control over the cost of workers' compensation insurance than they do over health insurance costs.

For one thing, workers' comp medical benefits are considered an entitlement, not an option, and insurers must pay the entire cost. Legislatures in many states set the levels of benefits that are paid to injured workers and insurance commissioners regulate the rates that insurers may charge to cover these benefits. This puts various medical-cost containment strategies, such as employee copayments and deductibles, off limits. What's more, while workers' comp is supposed to be a no-fault system, there has been an explosion in litigation in recent years. The best hope for an improved workers' compensation environment is for state legislatures to enact cost-containment reforms and for employers to improve their cost management programs. We describe some efforts along those lines below.

HOW WORKERS' COMPENSATION WORKS

Every state requires employers to assume medical costs employees incur when they get sick or injured as a result of their work, and to pay a proportion of wages. Employers are responsible for all medical costs and a percentage of wages—typically 67%, up to a maximum dollar limit.

Each state mandates matters such as employee eligibility requirements, rehabilitation procedures, and payment schedules, as well as requiring the employer to guarantee that it can meet all of its liabilities. Employers either meet this obligation by buying workers' compensation insurance or through other means.

In most states, workers' compensation coverage is provided through private insurance or through self-insurance arrangements. However, 20 states offer coverage through state funds and six of these require employers to use the state funds. Employer's premiums are based on risk.

Recent History

In the past decade, workers' compensation rates have risen more than twice as fast as the general inflation rate, says Richard Victor, executive director of the Workers' Compensation Research Institute in Cambridge, Massachusetts.

Benefits paid by insurers to injured workers tripled in the 1980s because of increases in medical costs, greater cash benefits, and a higher number of injuries and illnesses. Tillinghast, the insurance consulting division of New York-based Towers, Perrin, estimated that job-related injuries cost American employers over $60 billion in 1989 in direct workers compensation expenses.

In hazardous lines of work such as construction, trucking, manufacturing and outside service jobs, rates can be more than 10% of payroll.

Until recently, higher workers' compensation costs were driven primarily by ever-increasing cash benefits for injured workers, says John F. Burton, Jr., a Cornell University professor of labor economics and author of a bimonthly workers' compensation newsletter. "In the last few years, however, there has been a slowdown in cash benefit growth and medical expenses have become the driving force behind cost increases," says Burton.

In 1989 employers spent about $45 billion on workers' compensation insurance, almost double the figure of a decade before. The medical cost portion of that tab nearly doubled from $1,724 to $3,420 over that period, says the National Council on Compensation Insurance, and now accounts for about 41 percent of the total.

The rise in workers' compensation medical costs is compounded by the widening definition of work-related injury. Repetitive motion injuries and stress-related illness can be charged to workers' comp. The "VDT" disease—a cumulative trauma disorder caused by typing on a computer keyboard—has made workers' comp an office worker's issue.

Insurers have often avoided insuring small businesses as well as businesses in hazardous kinds of work. Insurers can argue that small businesses may not be able to afford the expense of keeping their working conditions safe. Small businesses also have low premium volumes.

In many states, insurance companies avoid selling unsurance to small businesses. As a result, many businesses are forced to buy their coverage through "assigned risk" pools, otherwise known as residual markets or markets of last resort.

In 1989 the assigned risk market accounted for about 20% of the total workers' compensation insurance market, making it the largest single provider of this kind of coverage in the country. In the state of Maine the assigned risk market accounted for the vast majority of the premiums.

SOLUTIONS

Self-Insurance

For larger sized businesses, one way to save on the high cost of workers' compensation insurance premiums is to self-insure. A 1990 Tillinghast survey of more than 500 employers reported that 42% self-insure, with 51% of companies with 7,000 or more employees self-insuring and 25% of those with fewer than 1,000 employees doing so. In addition, 25 states permit small companies to join group self-insurance plans.

If you are sure your workplace is safer than average, self-insurance is definitely worth considering.

Many companies band together in a group to buy stop-loss coverage for the truly big bills. Usually they join through the trade association that represents others in the same line of business, since the conventional wisdom is that the groups should all be in the same industry in order for the insurer to calculate the appropriate rates. As with conventional insurance, premiums will probably fluctuate based on the claims experience of the members of the group.

Needless to say, the decision to self-insure is not one to be taken lightly. While there may be no law in your state requiring you to buy health coverage for your employees, you have no choice under your state law about paying your employees' medical bills and paying for at least part of lost wages in the event of a disabling workplace injury. Make sure you have the financial resources to withstand potential losses.

Keeping Your Workplace Safe

Companies that self-insure have a keen interest in workplace safety, since they pay out of pocket to compensate for injuries due to workplace accidents. But any company whose workers' compensation insurance premiums will increase if it has excessive claims should be motivated to prevent accidents. While not every workplace injury can be anticipated and prevented, you can frequently lower your employees' risk of injury by changing the way they perform their jobs.

And we're not just talking about convincing workers to wear hard hats on construction sites or safety goggles in the steel plant. The United States has emerged as a service economy over the past two decades. Our workplace ailments have developed a distinct office flavor to them.

For example, a directory assistance operator or clerk using a word processor who spends hours forcefully typing on an awkwardly placed keyboard may find his wrists and fingers swollen, painful and tender. He has symptoms of tenosynovitis or tendonitis, in which the tendons in the wrists and hands become sore and inflamed.

The generic name for this and similar disorders is "cumulative trauma" or "repetitive motion" disorders and they occur in the factory too. A meatpacker who makes the same motions all day long and experiences tingling in her fingers and thumbs may be suffering from a condition known as carpal tunnel syndrome.

These kinds of disorders are a significant problem and are the most rapidly growing category of workplace issues, according to Roger Stephens, an industrial engineer/ergonomist for the Occupational Safety and Health Administration. In 1988, the Bureau of Labor Statistics reported 115,400 cases of cumulative trauma disorders, up 58% from the 72,900 cases it reported the year before.

How do you cope with these disorders? "The first thing employers should do is listen to their employees," said David J. Cochran, a professor of industrial and management systems engineering at the University of Nebraska in Lincoln. "Are they complaining about their jobs?"

Next, employers should look at their operations, facility by facility and job by job, examining job functions and injury and absentee rates of the employees performing those tasks.

Many employers, insurers, and ergonomics consultants say that videotaping workers can be extremely helpful in analyzing the risks involved in certain jobs. By running tapes in slow motion or stop-action, "employers can look for muscle stresses and work to redesign the equipment, modify the worker's position, or change the work flow," explained Theodore Braun, director of ergonomic services for Liberty Mutual Insurance Co. in Boston.

Modifying the workplace doesn't necessarily mean buying new equipment—just make the equipment you have more comfortable to work with. It can be as simple as raising chairs, slanting typing surfaces, or elevating work stations.

Sometimes the solution is obvious: Give employees a break from repetitive motion. "People engaged in high-intensity repetitive motion tasks should generally get more rest breaks than they do. Some attention should be paid to varying the job function, even if that means no more than going from one type of repetitive job to another," said David J. Eisen, research and information director for The Newspaper Guild, a union representing newspaper workers.

Sufferers from carpal tunnel syndrome who got that way from long hours of typing are advised to adjust the height of the chair and keyboard so that their elbows are bent at a roughly 90 degree angle. Also, take a break every hour to stretch the back, neck, arms, hands, and wrists, advises Dr. Linda Morse, director of occupational medicine at San Jose's Valley Health Center.

Cost Containment

As we mentioned earlier in the chapter, it's not as feasible to control workers comp costs as it is with health benefits because state legislatures and insurance commissioners often have the last word on the generosity of benefits. But things are changing.

Larger companies are beginning to use such cost-containment measures as auditing medical bills, reviewing physician practices, and pre-certifying hospital admissions, among other measures. Other companies check to make sure their workers comp coverage isn't duplicated by their regular medical insurance, and check doctors' rates against fee schedules in the states where such schedules exist.

"Many carriers and employers are developing workers' compensation programs which utilize managed care techniques commonly found in employee benefit medical plans," says Linda Sullivan, an actuary with the Boston office of TPF&C, the employee benefits consulting division of Towers, Perrin. These techniques include PPOs, utilization review and bill review.

"In addition, some employers are exploring the options of coordinating/integrating their short-term and long term disability plans with their workers' comp programs," Sullivan said. While the verdict isn't in yet on the potential of this approach, termed "24-hour coverage," you can expect to be hearing a lot more about it in the future.

FOR MORE INFORMATION

Organizations and Publications

The Workers' Compensation Research Institute, 245 First St., Cambridge, MA, 02142. A nonpartisan organization that publishes studies on the subject.

Analysis of Worker's Compensation Laws, 1991, U.S. Chamber of Commerce, $15. Write Publications Coordinator, U.S. Chamber of Commerce, 1615 H Street NW, Washington, D.C. 20062.

Worker's Compensation Insurance and Law Practice, The Next Generation, LRP Publications. An evaluation of current trends and dilemmas. Write 1035 Camphill Road, P.O. Box 579, Fort Washington, PA 19034.

CHAPTER 9

COMPLYING WITH THE AMERICANS WITH DISABILITIES ACT

The Americans with Disabilities Act (ADA), which was passed by Congress in the spring of 1990, is designed to make sure that businesses don't discriminate against the nation's 43 million disabled people—whether they're current or prospective employees or consumers of products and services.

Unless companies can show that they'd suffer undue hardship by doing so, most companies must accommodate handicapped employees and all of them must accommodate handicapped customers.

The law prohibits companies with 15 or more employees from citing a qualified job applicant's disability as the reason for not hiring the person. An employer has to accommodate the disabled person once he or she was hired—employing a reader for a blind employee, for example. Finally, all businesses have to make sure that public facilities such as rest rooms are accessible to the disabled.

Employers can face a lawsuit for turning down an applicant who can perform all the essential parts of a job but because of a disability can't perform an unessential duty traditionally included in the job description.

The new rules are to go into effect Jan. 26, 1992. Businesses with 25 or fewer employees will have an additional six months to comply and businesses with 10 or fewer workers will not be covered until Jan. 26, 1993.

The bill essentially extends the same protection established by the Civil Rights Act of 1964 against discrimination based on sex, religion, race, color, or national origin to people with physical or mental disabilities, including people with AIDS as well as recovering alcoholics and drug abusers.

Note the word "recovering" as it applies to drug and alcohol abusers. This doesn't mean that companies are no longer allowed to screen job applicants for illegal drug use. The law doesn't protect somebody who is a current user of illegal drugs, only rehabilitated individuals who are no longer users.

"Employers are permitted to conduct drug tests or take reasonable actions to ensure that an individual is no longer using illegal drugs," says the *Compliance Guide to the Americans With Disabilities Act*, published by the Small Business Legislative Council.

Small business won a few changes in the bill. The restaurant industry won an amendment that would permit restaurants to transfer an employee with a contagious disease or with AIDS to a job that doesn't involve food handling.

Small business also won a provision that says structural changes required to provide access for the disabled are the responsibility of landlords, not store owners who lease space. Another amendment says that although disabled people must be considered for employment if they can perform the essentials of a job, courts should consider a business owner's definition of a job when deciding what's necessary to perform it.

ACCOMMODATING EMPLOYEES

While a law firm might have to spend $20,000 to hire a reader to assist a blind attorney if the attorney is qualified to perform the work, most of the expenditures to accommodate disabled employees will be much less.

For the most part, the provisions covering hiring practices will not result in significant costs for small business, said John Satagaj, president of the Small Business Legislative Council, a coalition of trade groups with small-business members.

While some computer equipment for disabled workers is expensive, most state vocational rehabilitation organizations will pay all or part of the cost to help a company or an individual, say experts on the handicapped.

Businesses will have to rethink the way they interview job applicants, and decide whether the questions they ask are relevant, Satagaj said. "They'll have to put a little more thought into the upfront process."

Part of that process involves writing job descriptions. Barbara Judy, a project member of the Job Accommodation Network at the University of West Virginia, said she advises companies to break down the essential and unessential parts of each job description.

"I tell them to itemize all the things that the person did—break down each action—to see who can do what."

Larger companies that have a tradition of accommodating the handicapped have found that doing so needn't necessarily break the bank. Marriott Corp. employs more than 6,000 disabled employees in its 230,000-member worldwide workforce. Usually they're accommodated at no cost and 25% of the time the adjustment costs an average of $100.

At the Marriott restaurant in Philadelphia, then-manager Laura Davis was so impressed with the work of retarded and other disabled employees that she filled most of the staff with handicapped workers. In 1988 the restaurant was named Marriott's top unit.

Sears Roebuck & Co. says that 5.8%, or 20,300 of its 350,000 workers, have identified themselves as disabled. Most disabled employees are accommodated at no cost; about 10% need some help, at a typical cost of $20 to $350. Sears did pay $12,000 each for two machines that "look" at written material and read it aloud.

Some companies are going so far as to recruit disabled employees. The Bank of Montreal, for example, published a recruiting book in English and Braille. Honeywell Inc.'s Council on Honeywell Employees With Disabilities sponsored a symposium at which management-level people with such disabilities as deafness or post-polio mobility problems spoke about their jobs and the hurdles they had to overcome to get them.

Here are answers to common questions about complying with the employment portion of the ADA, adapted from *Compliance Guide to the Americans With Disabilities Act*, an excellent source of information on these matters.

Q: May I use physical criteria to describe a job's duties?

Yes, as long as that ability is necessary to the person's ability to perform the essential functions of the job in question. For example, a jewelry store seeking a security guard may require dexterity and mobility to perform the job because of the frequency of "snatch and run" thieves.

Q: Suppose my cafeteria is on the second floor. Am I supposed to provide access to disabled workers who work on the first floor?

The solution would probably be to provide a comparable space for the employee or employees on the first floor: coffee pot, tables and chairs, refrigerator, and enough space to eat with a coworker.

Q: Is this law similar to affirmative action? Do I have to favor the disabled applicant over the other applicants?

No, you are still free to select applicants for reasons unrelated to the disability. For example, religious entities may still give preference to people sharing a belief in their particular religious tenets.

Q: Am I still permitted to administer drug testing to prospective employees and to require applicants to take the test to be considered for employment?

Absolutely. Nothing in the law changes your ability to give a test to an applicant or a current employee or to refuse to hire an applicant or take action against the employee if the test accurately detects the presence of illegal drugs. However, you are not permitted to ask an applicant or employee whether they take prescription drugs under a doctor's supervision before a conditional offer of employment has been given. Nor can you give a test prior to this offer which would identify this fact. The easiest way to protect yourself and the prospective or current employee might be to give the test after the conditional offer of employment is made.

ACCOMMODATING CUSTOMERS

Businesses needn't necessarily spend a lot of money accommodating the handicapped; just be more accommodating, say experts on the law. One oft-cited example is that of the dry cleaner coming to the door of his shop to serve disabled patrons if widening the door would be too costly.

Most small storefront businesses can begin to comply with the law by installing ramps or widening doors for wheelchair users, experts say. An easy way to widen a doorway is by applying "swing clear" hinges that let a door swing back beyond a 90-degree angle when open, says the federal Architectural and Transportation Barriers Compliance Board.

Here are some examples of other low-cost accommodation measures: A grocery store wouldn't have to label its items in Braille but would be expected to train its employees to help the blind find what they need, according to drafters of the legislation. A bank probably wouldn't have to hire an interpreter to communicate with deaf customers but employees would be expected to write notes. And if the teller windows are too high, the bank would be expected to station an officer at a separate table to serve those in wheelchairs. Hotels would have to find ways to alert deaf and blind customers of an emergency. And restaurants would be required to rearrange tables rather than simply adopting the policy: "We don't serve wheelchairs."

"When they tell me that, I tell them, 'Good, I wasn't planning on ordering one,' " says Patrisha Wright, a lobbyist for the Disability Rights Education and Defense Fund.

There could be some significant expenses, however, particularly in the area of wheelchair accessibility. "Contrary to what proponents would like us to believe, not all of the costs are small," especially in comparison with the financial means of smaller companies, says John Motley, chief lobbyist for the National Federation of Independent Business. He says installing concrete wheelchair ramps costs between $1,000 and $10,000, widening an exterior door another $3,000, and hiring a certified sign-language interpreter about $23 an hour.

The National Association of Convenience Stores estimates it would cost $50,000 for an average store to widen its aisles to accommodate wheelchairs, lower display shelves, and make freezer cases usable by disabled persons.

Elevators must be installed in most buildings except those under three floors or with less than 3000 square feet per floor, other than in shopping centers and health care buildings.

There is some relief. Congress has enacted legislation that gives a construction tax credit of as much as $5,000 to companies with fewer than 30 employees and less than $1 million in annual sales, if they make physical improvements to their places of business to comply with the law.

FOR MORE INFORMATION

Publications

Compliance Guide to the Americans With Disabilities Act, Small Business Legislative Council, $14.25 each copy for orders of less than 25 copies. Discounts apply for larger orders and for council members. Provides a clearly written explanation of the law and provides examples of circumstances companies might have to deal with. Call (202) 639-8500 or write 1156 15th Street NW, Suite 510, Washington, D.C. 20005.

Organizations

Job Accommodation Network of America Inc., West Virginia University, P.O. Box 6122, Morgantown, WV 26506; (800) 526-7234. This group is considered an excellent resource for learning how to make reasonable accommodations for employees.

Mainstream Inc., 1030 15th Street NW, Washington, D.C. 20005; (202) 898-1400. Produces a newsletter that will update you on the specific regulations as they get promulgated. They also publish a number of reference guides. For example, one series, entitled "Putting Disabled People in Your Place: Focus on XXXXX (specific disability)," gives a background on mainstreaming an individual with a particular impairment, such as epilepsy.

The Equal Employment Opportunity Commission, 1800 L Street NW, Washington, D.C. 20507; (800) 872-3362. Will have responsibility for enforcing the employment part of the ADA.

The Architectural And Transportation Barriers Compliance Board, 400 Maryland Avenue SW, Washington, D.C. 20202; (202) 653-7834. Responsible for issuing the minimum guidelines and requirements for accessible design.

CHAPTER 10
DEALING WITH AIDS IN THE WORKPLACE

Which of the following examples exhibits the more enlightened business approach to the issue of acquired immune deficiency syndrome (AIDS)?

Example A: When a pizza maker at a Virginia fast-food restaurant fell ill, a rumor spread that he had AIDS. Soon after that, a vice president of the company fired the employee without notice. The man, who as it turned out didn't have AIDS, sued the company for discrimination and won since the company had no legal basis for its action.

Example B: When the president of a non-profit group in Washington, D.C. was informed that the group's public information director had been diagnosed as having AIDS, he quickly educated himself on AIDS in order to calm his confused staff. The president told the man he could work as long as he was able and launched a thorough AIDS education program for the company's 50 employees. Although the employee had to stop working three weeks later, he drew disability pay and received frequent visits from staff members, who consulted with him about the work in his department. Staff morale improved, and employees drew closer together as a result of the experience.

It seems obvious that the second example makes common sense, doesn't it? But you'd be amazed at not only how few small businesses have a plan in place to address the AIDS issue, but how many of their leaders have the wrong ideas about AIDS in the first place so they're dangerously ill-prepared to deal with the problem.

A shocking 75% of companies surveyed by the Philadelphia Commission on AIDS and the Greater Philadelphia Chamber of Commerce in 1988 knew little or nothing about their legal obligation to employees with AIDS. In addition, almost 40% said they would limit contact between employees with AIDS and co-workers; 16% indicated they would encourage workers infected with the virus to resign; and 30% said they would tell co-workers confidential information about workers with AIDS without their consent.

Ignorance about AIDS could result in dire consequences to the company: involvement in a lawsuit for one. Discrimination cases filed by workers with AIDS or AIDS- related complex against companies because they lost their jobs are mushrooming: In New York City, for example, there were three cases filed in 1983, 49 in 1984, 96 in 1985, 314 in 1986 and at least 549 in 1987. And these statistics were compiled before the enactment of the Americans With Disabilities Act in 1990. Because HIV-positive individuals are included within the law's definition of the handicapped, employers who fire workers because they have the virus that causes AIDS yet are able to work can be sued successfully for wrongful termination, attorneys say.

As a result, employers must treat employees who have the HIV virus as handicapped and provide appropriate accommodations whenever possible. The law, which we discussed at greater length in Chapter Nine, applies to all businesses with 15 or more employees.

About 10% of employers nationwide say they have had at least one employee with AIDS, according to a survey by Alexander & Alexander Consulting Group Inc. of Atlanta. The survey, based on 2,000 responses to a questionnaire mailed to 11,000 businesses, also said that 59% of the employers with more than 10,000 workers reported at least one AIDS case.

Larger corporations sharpened their focus on AIDS early in 1988 when 30 major employers endorsed a bill of rights that prevents discrimination in such areas as promotions, raises, or job assignments for AIDS victims. The ten-point code also commits its signers, which include IBM and AT&T, to educate their employees about the disease.

Some corporations don't fear the cost of the disease, they fear the effect that ignorance will have on productivity. Becky Padget, Atlanta-based Equifax's vice president of human resources, said that the company educates its workers about AIDS because "we were afraid of a mass walkout if people thought they were in danger of catching AIDS. We asked ourselves: 'Could we stay in business if there was a mass walkout?'—and the answer was no."

At worst, ignorance of the law can get you sued; at best, it can make your job difficult. Paul Kaplan, president of Northern Hills Office Services, a janitorial maintenance service company in Woodbury, New York, says many of his workers have refused to dispose of waste from medical facilities, even when they have strict infection-control procedures.

"They just won't do it," he says. "They're scared to death. The problem is rampant through my industry."

Some health economists argue that small businesses are less likely to employ HIV-infected workers than large companies because an increasing proportion of this population is made up of intravenous drug users, whose erratic work performance is more likely to get them dismissed from a smaller company. Even if this analysis is correct, we feel that small businesses should adopt a preemptive AIDS education program within their companies.

Small business owners need to know what they can and must do if an employee becomes infected with the virus, how to prevent discriminatory practices in the workplace, and how their employee benefit plans will be affected.

FACTS ABOUT AIDS

The first task for company management is to know the facts about AIDS in order to effectively communicate them to employees. According to the U.S. Public Health Service, the AIDS virus is very hard to catch; it is not spread by casual contact in schools, at parties, in swimming pools, stores or in the workplace.

AIDS is not transmitted by:

- Hugging, shaking hands, or simply being near a person who is infected with the virus
- Contact with toilet seats, showers or bathroom facili-ties
- Drinking from the same water fountain as an infected person
- Sharing telephones, typewriters, tools, and other equipment
- Eating in the same place or with the same utensils
- Sneezing, spitting, or coughing
- Coming into daily contact with an infected person

AIDS can be transmitted by:

- Having sex with an infected person
- Sharing needles and syringes with an infected person
- An infected mother to her baby during pregnancy or delivery
- Contact with the blood of an infected person

On the other hand, people with AIDS do typically suffer from respiratory diseases which are contagious and against which companies should exercise precautions, says James A. Klein, author of "AIDS: An Employer's Guidebook," produced by the Chamber of Commerce. (For more information on this and other resources, see the end of the chapter.)

"People afflicted with AIDS tend to suffer more frequently from various illnesses, especially respiratory diseases, that are contagious," says Klein, who is deputy executive director of the Association of Private Pension and Welfare Plans. "It is these secondary illnesses, not AIDS itself, that may pose a health risk in the workplace. Employers and co-workers should take appropriate precautions."

LAWS COMPANIES MUST OBSERVE

The second task for management is to understand the laws that protect AIDS-infected workers.

Mandatory job screening tests for AIDS or HIV is illegal in some states. Even in states where it's not illegal, it is the subject of moral and ethical dispute and may put a company in legal jeopardy. What's more, the tests aren't 100% accurate and may fail to give any useful information. For that reason, companies should beware of using an insurance carrier's test requirements or coverage refusal as a screening technique.

There simply aren't a lot of legally valid reasons for refusing to hire people because they have AIDS. Fear that employees won't want to work with the person, high insurance costs, and adverse public reaction aren't good enough reasons.

Workers with AIDS are recognized as handicapped under the law and are therefore entitled to protection. They cannot be fired because they have AIDS; in fact the law requires that employers make various accommodations for workers with AIDS, just as they do for any disabled employee.

The employer is required to make "reasonable accommodation" for an "otherwise qualified" employee's limitations. The exact meaning of these phrases is up for grabs but Anita Schoomaker, an attorney with Morgan, Lewis & Bockius who represents management in labor cases, gives her version. "If an employee is physically able to do the job but needs an adjustment in his schedule because he has to work later hours, and the shop is open later, the employer is obliged to accommodate that schedule."

Health experts also point out that people under treatment for an HIV infection can remain productive employees for years after the first symptoms appear. Even people with the "end stage" of an HIV infection can remain productive for much of their illness.

If an employee becomes unable to continue to work at previous levels of productivity, state laws generally don't require an employer to move an employee with AIDS to a different, less strenuous job within the company, although employers may try to make that accommodation.

Here are typical accommodations for employees with AIDS who are still on the job: modify their duties, give them time off for medical appointments; reduce their workload; let them work at home via computer; give them frequent rest periods; transfer them to a less strenuous job.

"Employers need to be sensitive to the fact that continued employment for an employee with any life-threatening illness may sometimes be therapeutically important in their recovery process and may possibly prolong the employee's life," advises the excellent booklet, *AIDS: Its Impact on Your Business*, published by the Philadelphia Commission on AIDS and the Greater Philadelphia Chamber of Commerce. (For information on how to get the booklet and others, see the end of the chapter.)

What's more, you may not have the legal right to fire the individual, according to the publication. "Due to the protected physical handicap status of AIDS, employers can't make employment and retention decisions based on AIDS infection. As long as the employee can still perform the job, he or she can't be disciplined or terminated because of the AIDS infection."

However, the laws don't require an employer to accommodate the handicapped person by modifying the job from full-time to part-time unless the business has several part-time employees doing that job. "It has to be decided on a case-by-case basis," says labor attorney Anita Schoomaker. "There's no easy rule of thumb."

Employers are required to keep confidential any medical information they have about any employee. Violating the privacy of an AIDS victim can be cause for legal action. An employee can volunteer medical information but no company can force its disclosure. An employee's right to confidentiality is considered violated if the employer asks him to inform others of his illness.

This leads to the issue of how a manager or supervisor judiciously handles queries from employees about whether a co-worker has AIDS. Ira Singer of the Nova Health Care Group suggests answering: "Joe seems to be sick, but all medical information is strictly confidential. I hope you'd respect his privacy."

Singer also suggests talking with the affected employee, however, to see if he wants to participate in an AIDS education group or wants his co-workers to know. We'll deal more with the education process below.

Even speculation by an employer or co-workers that an employee may have AIDS may be grounds for libel or slander suits. As we illustrated in the example that began this chapter, this is a mistake that no company can afford to make.

A company can't fire an employee because he has AIDS, or isolate him from his co-workers, or otherwise behave toward him in a way that discriminates against him because of his illness. There is one exception: An amendment to the Americans With Disabilities Act says that employees with AIDS or other infectious diseases who handle food may be reassigned to a different job for which they are qualified.

This amendment got passed despite insistence on the part of health authorities that AIDS can't be transmitted through food handled by an infected employee. According to "AIDS and Your Job—Are There Risks?," a report by the American Red Cross and the U.S. Public Health Service, "Because the AIDS virus is not transmitted in food, people who work with food, such as cooks, caterers, waiters, bartenders, airline attendants, and others should not be restricted from work because they have AIDS or have been infected with the AIDS virus." Of course, health experts say that infected workers with open sores, skin lesions, or other illnesses for which any food handlers would also be restricted should be restricted from work.

On the other hand, employers are not obligated to retain an AIDS-infected employee once that person can no longer do the job. The Americans With Disabilities Act makes accommodations for the fact that companies are in the business of making money, not caring for sick people. It is the employer's decision how much he or she wants to keep the AIDS-afflicted worker on the payroll once the person becomes too ill to work.

GUIDELINES TO HELP EMPLOYERS DEAL WITH AIDS

The Citizens Commission on AIDS for New York City and Northern New Jersey has formulated guidelines to help employers deal with AIDS. The recommendations, "Responding to AIDS: Ten Principles for the Workplace," has been endorsed by more than 360 companies and organizations. Here is a summary of the bill of rights.

- People with AIDS or HIV infection are entitled to the same rights as other employees.
- Employment policies must comply with the law.
- Employment policies must be based on the evidence that people with AIDS don't pose a risk of transmitting the virus to other workers.

- Management and union leadership alike should endorse nondiscriminatory employment policies and education policies.
- Employers and unions should communicate their support of these policies clearly.
- Employers should provide employees with sensitive, accurate and up-to-date education about risk reduction in their personal lives.
- Employers have a duty to protect the confidentiality of employees' medical information.
- Employers should undertake education for all employees before a problem occurs, in order to prevent work disruption and rejection of an HIV-infected employee by co-workers.
- Employers should not require HIV screening as part of pre-employment screening.
- In an occupational setting where there may be a potential risk of exposure to the HIV virus, employers should take precautions, provide protective equipment, and offer specific and ongoing education.

Recommendations for Certain Categories of Workers

The Centers for Disease Control has issued recommendations to help employers understand the health risks to certain categories of workers and to adopt safety precautions. The CDC addresses both the risks of employees spreading AIDS and the risks of employees catching AIDS. These recommendations note:

In general: An employee with AIDS need not be restricted from work unless there is evidence of another illness that would restrict him from performing the job. Employees with AIDS have no known risk of transmitting the virus to co-workers, customers, or consumers.

Food service workers: Cooks, waiters, bartenders, and airline attendants don't pose a risk of contamination since there isn't evidence of transmitting the virus through food. (Although, as we mentioned above, an amendment to the Americans With Disabilities Act permits the transfer of AIDS-infected workers to a different area.) Workers should follow standard practices of good hygiene. Avoid injuries that might contaminate the food with blood. Discard food that does become contaminated.

Personal service workers: Barbers, hairdressers, and cosmetologists don't need to exercise special precautions. People who use needles or other instruments that pierce the skin should discard the instruments after use or clean and thoroughly sterilize them before re-use.

Health care workers: Health care workers run the greatest risk of being exposed to the AIDS virus—particularly those involved in surgery—and in passing it on to others. The Centers for Disease Control (CDC) recommends that all health care workers wear protective garments, wash exposed areas thoroughly, use mouthpieces and resuscitation bags, and use special care in handling laboratory waste.

EDUCATING EMPLOYEES

The third task is to educate employees about the disease, creating a pre-emptive strike against the most dangerous manifestations of ignorance: fear and hysteria.

Take, for example, Ben Strohecker, owner of an auto dealership in Salem, Massachusetts, who has 150 mostly part-time workers, none of whom has contracted AIDS. But he has sponsored an employee-wide education program during the workday three times in the three years he has been in business.

He called on the local Red Cross chapter, which provides an hour-long workplace AIDS education program for $10 per person. Strohecker says he started the program "out of fear and my own ignorance of the disease and its accompanying issues. I believed that I as the owner had to be the one to stand up and do something."

The employees' response pleased him. "The sessions are explicit. I thought some people might walk out. But the response was heartening."

Experts say that employers can take a variety of communication approaches, either by putting informational material in pay envelopes, sending it to employees at home, posting information on bulletin boards, or supplying it at staff meetings.

Information should be provided in a number of different ways and repeated at least five times before the message gets through. On a subject like AIDS, which is emotionally and culturally fraught, there can be great resistance to information; facts must be delivered in various forms and over a period of time if the resistance to them is to be overcome.

Workers who only get brochures from companies about the disease and nothing else are more likely to have negative feelings towards AIDS-affected colleagues than employees who get no information, says Georgia Tech researcher David Herold.

Here are some case histories of companies with successful education programs. For more information on how to set up your own, consult the organizations list at the end of this chapter.

Case History Number One:

Pacific Bell's education program started by Chuck Woodman, supervisor of operations at the Baby Bell, has been called "a model of intelligent action" by AIDS experts. Woodman considers himself an unlikely supporter of people with AIDS; he's a devout Mormon, father of eight, and admirer of tough guys like John Wayne and George Patton. But after a worker under his supervision died of AIDS and he heard the minister at the funeral talk about how angry it made him feel that people with AIDS are shunned, "The whole moral question of homosexuality got put aside."

The utility had already confronted ignorance about the disease from other employees. One coin collector wouldn't touch phone booths in predominantly gay neighborhoods in San Francisco. The members of a Los Angeles phone installation crew balked at working in a hospice where people were afflicted with AIDS. A lineman refused to use the truck of a fellow employee rumored to have died of AIDS until it was sterilized. So Woodman and Michael Eriksen, then the company's director of preventive medicine, started an AIDS Education Task Force.

As a result of the task force's efforts, in 1986 the company helped sponsor the first conference on AIDS in the workplace and produced the first video aimed at business people which explores the medical evidence and emotional issues in great detail. The video was such a success that it was subsequently aired on public television and in France and Japan.

Case History Number Two:

In the book *AIDS: Its Impact on Your Business,* the Philadelphia Commission on AIDS gave this account of the education effort of one local restaurant after a waiter who had been ill notified the manager that he was HIV infected. The restaurant manager first became aware of misgivings on the part of the other employees about working with the infected man when he decided to return to work after taking a month's leave of absence.

The manager then decided to hold mandatory education meetings for the restaurant's 50 employees, calling in an AIDS education expert who spoke about:

• Transmission of the disease and how it is and isn't spread.

• Prevention—how to avoid contacting the virus.

• Confidentiality—why an employee is entitled to keep medical information confidential.

The employees also viewed videotapes and received written materials. At the end of the sessions, employees were encouraged to ask questions or to telephone the expert later. A questionnaire was distributed to ascertain whether the session was helpful; all but two who attended said it was.

Was the effort a success? Some might say no: One of the employees quit because he said he didn't want to work with an HIV-infected person. On the other hand, if the restaurant hadn't decided to take a "pro-active" education approach rather than saying and doing nothing, it's likely that many more employees would have quit and morale would have been low among those who didn't.

Case History Number Three:

In the mid-1980s, panic swept a General Motors plant in Clinton, Mississippi when word leaked out that a worker had been diagnosed with AIDS. Other workers refused to use bathrooms or phones that the AIDS sufferer had touched; some even threatened to stay home if the infected employee returned to work. That kind of scare is unlikely to happen again. Spurred by the incident, the company and the United Auto Workers launched a $2 million program to allay concerns about the disease and to safeguard the rights of AIDS victims.

"AIDS is not a threat to the workplace," said GM's Patricia Houtteman, who is co-director of AIDS education. "The fear of it is."

GM has mailed brochures and magazines on AIDS to all of its 500,000 employees and their families and provided classes for workers on the spread, prevention, and treatment of the disease. Through teleconferencing, seminars, and written materials, the auto giant trains plant managers, union officials, health personnel, and counselors to deal with everything from discrimination against AIDS victims to safety issues. GM allows AIDS-infected employees to stay on the job as long as they are physically able to do the work.

Other Examples:

Digital Equipment Corp. has organized dialogues between individuals with the disease and groups of healthy employees. When an employee died of AIDS not long ago, the company brought in trauma intervention teams to counsel fellow workers.

Another pioneer, Levi Strauss, offers terminally ill AIDS patients home and hospice care as a compassionate and cost-efficient alternative to long-term hospitalization. But the company also encourages sick employees to keep working through flexible schedules and part-time jobs and counsels them and their families on such topics as handling rumors and returning to work.

INSURANCE COVERAGE AND MEDICAL TREATMENT

When Larry J., operator of a Los Angeles movie theater, was diagnosed as carrying the AIDS virus in 1987, his health insurance premiums went up from $540 per month to $1,800—about half the profits of the theater.

While AIDS claims currently account for only about 1% of the total life, accident and health claims tallied by insurers, that number will grow. The cost of direct medical care for the 91,000 new cases expected in 1991 will total $6 billion over the patients' lifetimes, or more than $60,000 per case, according to the National Center for Health Services and Health Technology Assessment. Those figures grow to $7.5 billion for the 114,000 expected new cases in 1992.

Currently the cost of care for the average AIDS case is manageable: one-third that of a heart attack victim, health experts say. The grim fact is that once diagnosed as having AIDS, few patients live longer than three years. Those years are typically spent going in and out of hospitals, as patients find themselves unable to shake off diseases such as pneumonia.

Is AIDS having an effect on insurance premiums? Not yet, says Warren Greenberg, a health economist at George Washington University. "We should be cautious as to whether or not it will precipitate premium increases in the future," because many people with AIDS aren't covered by private insurance plans but are unemployed or on public assistance.

But this scenario is rapidly changing. The medical costs of government programs have been shifted onto insurers as the government adopts its own cost controls. What's more, "improved survival rates and more aggressive high-tech outpatient treatments are driving lifetime costs up," said Jon Eisenhandler, an AIDS statistics expert at Empire Blue Cross/Blue Shield.

However, using techniques such as case management discussed in Chapter Three, studies have shown that cost containment can be effective. Case management is not only relevant to you if you pay your employees' medical bills out of pocket—that is, you "self-insure" these bills—but if you pay insurance premiums as well, since companies whose insurance policies are experience-rated will find their insurance premiums skyrocketing if they start running up big health bills because of AIDS.

Here's an example of case management supplied by the Philadelphia Commission on AIDS: Instead of being admitted to a hospital, a man with AIDS decided to get care at home, since his roommate was willing to provide his care for 12 hours a day. After meeting with the attending physician, a nurse coordinator hired by the insurance company presented a home care plan that involved arranging for a nurse in the home four hours a day and volunteers from the local AIDS support group the rest of the time. Besides permitting the patient to remain in familiar and comfortable surroundings, $32,250 was saved by opting to provide the man's care at home.

DISABILITY AND LIFE INSURANCE COVERAGE

A major portion of insurance costs associated with people with AIDS seems to be not so much in providing health care but in providing income replacement, i.e., paying out disability benefits and life insurance, especially for high-salaried professionals.

Some insurance experts believe that ultimately life insurance premiums will go up because of increased claims. And, at the same time the product becomes more expensive and therefore less attractive as a benefit to small employers, employees may demand it as a benefit because individual policies will become harder to obtain in the "marketplace."

In the meantime, insurers will try to keep costs down by screening for AIDS, and in some cases by requiring employees to complete an "evidence of insurability" form if they elect to increase their life insurance coverage to more than a certain multiple of their annual salary. Insurers may also make it more costly to buy insurance with a "waiver of premium" feature which permits totally disabled people to continue life insurance without paying any more premiums.

Like other insurance costs, disability expenses are likely to rise as more active workers begin to suffer the effects of AIDS. Also, as better medical treatments prolong the lives of AIDS patients, the lengths of AIDS disabilities may be extended, adding to costs. Since these policies represent a percentage of lost wages, disability costs are greater for higher-income employees who are disabled, and that would be reflected in the premiums.

Johnson & Higgins, a benefits consulting firm in New York, came up with its own estimates of the employer cost when two different hypothetical employees were disabled and then died because of AIDS. For a person making $25,000, the employer's cost for medical, disability, life insurance, and retirement benefits could range from $98,000 to $198,000, the firm says. For an employee with a salary of $75,000, these benefit costs could range from $215,000 to $315,000.

People in the advanced stage of AIDS will be unable to work for periods of time. A disability policy that permits people to return to work periodically or work at home may be mutually beneficial, especially for professional employees, offering the employee financial protection and the employer reduced costs. Types of policies that provide this coverage are the "zero day residual" policies or loss-of-income policies, which we discussed in Chapter Seven. Check with your insurer for details.

FOR MORE INFORMATION

Publications

AIDS: An Employer's Guidebook, U.S. Chamber of Commerce. Gives an excellent overview of the disease, employee benefit considerations, legal issues concerning AIDS, and tips on conducting an education program. Write Publications Fulfillment, 1615 H Street NW, Washington, D.C. 20006.

AIDS: Its Impact on Your Business, Philadelphia Commission on AIDS. Addresses workplace issues and education. Call (212) 898-4750 or write the Leonard Davis Institute of Health Economics, University of Pennsylvania, 3641 Locust Walk, Philadelphia, PA 19104-6218.

AIDS Education: A Business Guide; AIDS Information Directory; both by the American Foundation for AIDS Research. Call (212) 719-0033 or write 1515 Broadway, Suite 3601, New York, NY 10036-8901.

Guide to Services and Information, Personnel Journal. The periodical maintains a list of publications, videotapes and training manuals related to AIDS in the workplace, running an education program and developing a corporate AIDS policy. Call (714) 751-1883 or write 245 Fischer Ave., B-2, Costa Mesa, CA 92626.

What All Businesses Really Need to Know About AIDS, 3-page brochure, United Way of America. Businesses can reprint the brochure in bulk with their own company logo. Write 701 N. Fairfax St., Alexandria, VA 22314.

Organizations

American Red Cross. Your local Red Cross chapter can make a speaker available and provide informational videotapes that address workplace issues such as confidentiality, casual contact with infected workers, and employee responses to the occurrence of AIDS.

The National AIDS Information Clearinghouse, P.O. Box 6003, Rockville, MD 20850; (800) 458-5231.

The National Leadership Coalition on AIDS, 1150 17th Street NW, Suite 202, Washington, D.C. 20036; (202) 872-1977.

The Small Business Response to the AIDS Project, c/o Nova HealthCare Group, 7661 Provincial Drive, Suite 209, McLean, VA 22102.

National AIDS Network, 1012 14th Street NW, Suite 601, Washington, D.C. 20005; (202) 347-0390. Can direct you to local organizations that provide educational programs or direct services to people with AIDS.

CHAPTER 11
DRUG TESTING, DRUG TREATMENT

A driver for Sawyer Gas Co. in Jacksonville, Florida was fired after admitting he had used marijuana the day he drove a liquid-gas tank truck into a ditch. The truck didn't explode and the driver wasn't injured, but company owner Charlie Sawyer was so concerned about the incident that he set out to educate himself about drugs.

Sawyer said that he and his wife, Joanne, found "reams of information" on drugs and drug abuse but no formal program for employers. So Sawyer Gas started "Knowledge is Power," an anti-drug program for its employees.

Businesses throughout Jacksonville learned about the Sawyers' program and in 1989 it became the prototype for an anti-drug program called "Put Drugs Out of Business," sponsored by the Jacksonville Chamber of Commerce, of which Sawyer is now chairman and CEO.

A local firm developed a slick print and video package for the campaign, donating employee time and materials estimated at $150,000. The program has been adopted by about 300 companies and is governed by business leaders, politicians, law enforcement officials, students—and even former drug dealers with insiders' views on the problems.

UNCLE SAM MAY WANT YOU TO FIGHT DRUGS

Small businesses that don't want to bother with a drug education program because it's too costly or an administrative burden should think again—especially if they do any business with the government. A recently passed federal law, the Drug Free Workplace Act, shifts the responsibility of an employee's substance abuse onto the shoulders of the employer if that employer has a government contract for $25,000 or more or a federal grant of any size.

If the employer doesn't make a "good faith effort" to establish programs that can create a drug-free workplace, the company can be disqualified for up to five years from even bidding on a government contract.

Here are the employer's responsibilities:

- Publish a statement notifying employees of its policy regarding a drug-free workplace. Inform employees that unlawful manufacturing, distribution, sale, possession, or use of a controlled substance is prohibited and that action will be taken against violators.
- Distribute that policy to employees.
- Establish a drug-free awareness program.

- Notify the federal agency with which it has a contract in the event of any employee's drug conviction at the workplace. Inform employees that as a condition of employment they must notify the employer within five days of any conviction of a drug violation that occurred in the workplace. The employer must notify the contracting agency within ten days of a conviction.

THE THREAT IN THE WORKPLACE

But even those employers who don't routinely do business with the federal government have reason to be concerned about the toll that drug abuse takes in the workplace. "Drug trafficking is the most serious organized crime problem in the world today," said The President's Commission on Organized Crime, which argued that the government and private companies can play a vital role in curbing demand for drugs.

The Commission asked all U.S. companies to test for drug use in 1986. In an initial report based on a 32-month study, the commission urged the government not only to test its own workers but to withhold federal contracts from private firms that refuse to do the same.

Civil libertarians in Congress objected. Said Charles Schumer, (D-NY), "Trying to stop organized crime's multimillion dollar drug business by creating a police state in federal office buildings would be virtually ineffective and would create one crime to stop another."

While labor, management, and politicians continue to wrangle over the ethics and legality of drug testing, nobody argues about the extent of the damage drugs do to business. The consequences range from accidents and injuries to theft, bad decisions, and ruined lives. Drug abusers are three times as likely as nonusers to injure themselves or someone else. Moreover, addicts with expensive habits are much more likely to steal cash from a company safe, products from a warehouse, or equipment from a factory.

Federal experts estimate that between 10% and 23% of all U.S. workers use dangerous drugs on the job. And there's plenty of evidence that taking drugs on the job isn't a victimless crime. Since 1975, at least 50 train accidents have been attributed to drug or alcohol impaired workers. In those mishaps, 53 people were killed and more than $34 million worth of property was destroyed. In 1987, for example, a Conrail/Amtrak train wreck in Maryland that killed 16 people was apparently caused by employee drug abuse.

Employers are clearly sick and tired of paying the insurance cost of employees who can't work because of injuries caused by drug use. In addition to the Maine legislature, which modified a highly restrictive law passed in 1989, Florida, Oregon and Georgia recently revised their workers' compensation laws to limit the benefits workers can claim when injured because of drug use.

Not surprisingly, younger workers abuse drugs more than their older counterparts, with marijuana being the drug of choice, according to Kaim Associates, Inc., a consulting firm in Weston, Connecticut specializing in information services for the health care industry. According to the survey, released in 1990, 8% of all fulltime employees use drugs at least once a month, of which 87.5% use marijuana. But that's taking into account all workers. Among those aged 18 to 25, the incidence of illegal drug use is double that of the workforce as a whole: 19% of full-time employees in this age group use drugs at least once a month.

Whereas many executives took a hands-off approach to workplace drug abuse during the 1970s when the prevailing political attitude was "don't invade my space," the pro-business sentiments of the 1980s produced a much harder line against drug abuse. Says Capital Cities/ABC President Daniel Burke: "I consider drugs damn dangerous. I believe that my responsibility is such that my position against drugs has to be clearly understood by everyone who works under my direction."

What's more, employees themselves are concerned about drugs in the workplace and are grateful when management takes action. In a poll conducted for the Institute for a Drug Free Workplace, 82% of employees surveyed said they support company policies against drug abuse and favor disciplinary action for violations of such policies.

Drug experts recommend a four-step action plan to combat drugs in the workplace:

- Determine whether one or more of your employees is a drug abuser.
- Discuss with the employee what action will be taken to address the problem, both the rehabilitative measures to treat the abuse problem and the disciplinary measures to be taken if work performance doesn't improve. Then keep your word.
- Implement a drug testing policy company-wide.
- Implement a drug treatment program—either in-house for larger companies, or by referral.

STEP ONE: DETERMINE IF THERE IS A PROBLEM

Your first task is to determine whether you've got a drug abuser or abusers in your workforce. There are telltale signs—and the bottom line is reduced productivity. A study conducted by Workplace Consultants Inc. says that the abuser is three times as likely to be late for work, uses three times as much sick time and is involved in employee theft ten times as often.

Other telltale signs of use: If an employee uses the rest room often and doesn't work up to his full potential, there's a good chance he's using marijuana or cocaine, says Charles R. Carroll, a consultant who specializes in drug abuse in the workplace. If the employee's eyes are red and his physical appearance declines, there's a good chance of some kind of substance abuse. Frequently missed deadlines or an increase in mistakes are tip-offs. While employees can use breath mints to cover up the smell of alcohol, there's one area they can't cover up: work performance.

STEP TWO: TAKE ACTION

You don't have to have a drug program in place to let an employee know gently but firmly that he's got to shape up or ship out. If you find an employee's performance slipping, it's time to call a conference and let him or her know. "Ask the person why it's happening, but no matter what the answer is, you should stick to a deadline by which the employee must return to his old level of performance," says Carroll.

Should the performance not improve, it's time for a second conference, Carroll says. This one should include another person—this time someone from personnel, if your company has such a department, or in a supervisory position. The employee should be warned that unless there's a change in performance, he or she may be suspended or even terminated.

Sometimes the caring handling of a problem employee will elicit the confession that the employee has a problem, says Carroll. At this point, he needs help. The local chapter of Alcoholics Anonymous can be of assistance, as well as the National Association of State Alcohol and Drug Abuse Directors.

You also have to decide what disciplinary action will be taken if you don't see improvement: Your choices can include dismissal, suspension with or without pay, demotion, transfer, and/or an offer of rehabilitation or counseling.

Be careful to document as fully as possible a relationship between declining job performance and drug abuse before taking disciplinary action against an employee, experts say. This is especially important for employees in jobs where there is minimal risk to the safety of the public or coworkers, little need for public trust, or no access to substantial amounts of cash or valuables.

Mark de Bernardo, executive director of the Washington, D.C.-based Institute for a Drug Free Workplace, believes that workers with chronic drug abuse problems should be dismissed. By chronic he means "those who are unable or unwilling to be rehabilitated; those who pose a significant safety or security risk; those who can't do the job they were hired to do as a result of drug use or those who have been apprehended selling drugs on the job."

De Bernardo says that if you tell people there will be consequences of inappropriate behavior they'll usually either change the behavior or take it somewhere else. "It's behavior modification. If you raise the level of user accountability, the user will either change his behavior or he'll leave (to find another job) because he likes to get high."

STEP THREE: DRUG TESTING

Your next step is to decide whether to implement a drug testing policy—and whether to restrict it to new hires or to include all employees. Your employees may be more receptive than you think; see Figures 11-1 and 11-2.

Figure 11-1

Drug Testing is a...
"Good Idea"
...say American Workers

From workers in safety-sensitive jobs to office workers, a strong majority of American employees think "periodic drug testing" is a "good idea."

When asked if they thought it is a good idea or a bad idea to drug test workers in certain occupations, the 1,007 full-time employees surveyed by the Gallup Organization overwhelmingly supported drug testing.

For those employees in safety-sensitive jobs, 93 percent of American workers think it is a good idea to require periodic drug screening tests. When asked about factory workers, 73 percent favored drug testing. Even for office workers, 61 percent of those polled thought it was a good idea to have regular drug testing.

American workers favor drug testing for themselves as well. When asked about workers in *their own* occupation, 69 percent stated that drug testing is appropriate.

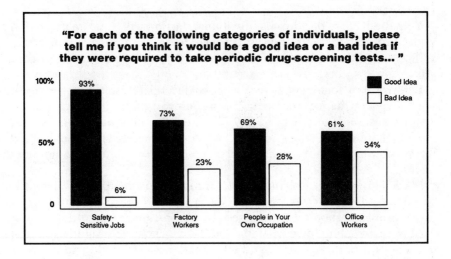

Who Was Surveyed?

- 1,007 full-time workers, 18 years of age or older, working outside of the home

- 82% were between the ages of 25 and 54.

- The survey was regionally stratified to be representative of the American population as a whole.

Methodology

- Gallup randomly conducted telephone interviews and had responsibility for insuring that all items were technically correct and without bias.

- All field work was validated at the 10% level by supervisory callbacks.

- The margin of error was plus or minus 3.1%.

Figure 11-2

State Surveys Show Overwhelming Support for Drug Testing

G allup asked 500 employees in twelve separate state surveys if they think drug testing is a good idea or a bad idea for employees in safety-sensitive jobs, factories, offices, and *"your own* occupation." In almost every category in every state a majority of workers strongly support drug testing.

Workers in Safety-Sensitive Jobs

	Good Idea	Bad Idea
Delaware	95	5
Texas	94	4
Illinois	94	6
Indiana	94	6
Florida	93	6
Montana	93	6
New York	93	6
Wisconsin	93	6
California	92	7
Connecticut	92	7
Washington	91	8
Arizona	89	8

Factory Workers

	Good Idea	Bad Idea
Texas	84	13
Illinois	76	20
Delaware	76	21
Florida	76	21
Indiana	74	22
Montana	74	22
New York	72	24
Wisconsin	72	25
California	70	24
Arizona	69	22
Washington	68	26
Connecticut	66	30

People in *Your Own* Occupation

	Good Idea	Bad Idea
Texas	77	20
Indiana	73	24
Illinois	71	26
Florida	70	27
Arizona	69	23
Delaware	69	27
Montana	68	29
Wisconsin	67	31
New York	66	30
California	65	33
Washington	61	34
Connecticut	61	35

Office Workers

	Good Idea	Bad Idea
Texas	68	27
Indiana	65	31
Illinois	62	34
Arizona	61	29
Florida	61	34
Delaware	60	36
Wisconsin	57	39
Montana	56	36
New York	55	41
Washington	52	41
California	50	45
Connecticut	48	48

INSTITUTE for a
DRUG-FREE
WORKPLACE

For more information on the Institute for a Drug-Free Workplace, write:
P.O. Box 65708, Washington, D.C. 20035-5708; or call (202) 828-4590.

11/90

A practice which was virtually unheard of at the dawn of the 1980s, drug testing has become a common employer practice, as concern grows about the effect substance abuse has on productivity.

Tom Warner, the president of Warner Corp., a northeast Washington plumbing business with about 220 employees, was attending a Washington, D.C. Board of Trade seminar in 1985 when he got a clue as to why his company had trouble keeping young employees.

Warner said he couldn't figure out why his employees had so many accidents—and why 75% of his apprentices didn't stick out their training program to become full-time employees. When he heard the effects of drugs on workers and the workplace, "It made it clear that so many of our problems were drug-related," he said.

By making a commitment to make his company a drug-free workplace, things started to change. But drug testing was the key. Although it cost him at least $7,500 a year, it saves a bundle in insurance and training costs.

"Once we started screening, it was like night and day," Warner said. "Everybody stayed. It was a dramatic change in the company."

More and more firms are requiring job applicants to undergo urinalysis. Says Peter Bensinger, a former head of the Drug Enforcement Agency who is now a consultant: "Companies do have a right and responsibility to establish sound working conditions. We're talking about people and their safety and our own individual rights to work in a safe environment."

In 1983 only 3% of all major corporations had drug testing programs. By 1988 that number exceeded 50%. Although less common for small and medium sized businesses, drug testing is nonetheless widespread.

The most common type of drug test uses a urine specimen. The specimen is divided in half so that a confirming test can be done on the second portion if the first test comes out positive. By mixing it with a chemical that reacts to a specific drug, the laboratory can detect marijuana, cocaine, heroin and other illegal and legal drugs.

The cost of drug screening will vary depending on the method use and the number of drugs tested for. The National Institute on Drug Abuse (NIDA) certifies certain labs to do testing. We've included information about how to contact the institute at the end of the chapter.

How reliable is drug testing? Initial screening can result in some false positives or negatives. But the second confirming test, using gas chromatography or mass spectrometry, is virtually free of error, experts say.

Is it legal to require new hires to be drug free? A qualified "yes." There is no U.S. constitutional prohibition against drug testing in the private sector. If and when the Constitution's ban on unreasonable searches is interpreted to cover drug testing, experts say, it would only apply to the public sector, not to private employers.

Needless to say, extreme caution must be taken to make sure there are no state laws that prohibit testing and to make sure the tests are conducted properly.

Mark de Bernardo of the Institute for a Drug-Free Workplace recommends requesting—but not requiring—job applicants to sign a waiver of legal rights of action against the employer for administering drug tests and acting in "good faith" on the results. Such a release must be signed knowingly and willingly.

Should you adopt a drug-testing policy? Some experts say you should take the plunge if it looks like you already have a problem. Increases in absenteeism, accidents, workers' compensation claims, turnover, thefts of company property, and arrests are a few tip-offs. Even a drop in productivity can be linked to drug abuse.

Others say you can't wait until you detect a problem because you won't necessarily be able to spot it.

"Most employers don't know how to or are unwilling to recognize a problem," says Susan Berger, who directs the Washington, D.C.-based Small Business Project at the Corporation Against Drug Abuse in Washington, D.C., a non-profit group that deals with workplace drug abuse issues in the District.

If you decide to adopt a drug testing policy, drug experts say you have to decide who will be tested: all job applicants, all employees, just employees with safety and security responsibilities, or just those who have had accidents. A certain Midwest utility will only test employees for drug use in four situations: when there is probable cause, for pre-employment screening, during or after an employee's participation in a substance abuse rehabilitation program, and when hiring company drivers, as required by the law in that state.

A chain of do-it-yourself stores tests employees for drug use in cases involving probable cause; after a worker is involved in a serious workplace accident; after participation in a rehabilitation program; and when an employee is a candidate for a promotion. The company dismisses employees with fewer than two years of service who test positive for drug use. Employees with two or more years of service can keep their jobs if they undergo treatment paid for partially by the company's major medical insurance program.

STEP FOUR: TREATMENT PROGRAMS

To help put impaired workers on the road to rehabilitation, about 30% of the Fortune 500 largest industrial corporations have established in-house employee assistance programs, commonly known as EAPs. Many of these programs were set up during the 1970s for workers suffering from alcoholism, and have since been expanded to include drug abusers. The motivation behind the EAPs has been economic as well as humanitarian. It's much easier to help a person who has been on the job for years than it is to hire and train someone to replace him.

Here's how a drug treatment program typically operates at a large company: Employees with a problem can call or stop by the medical department. Or supervisors who spot unusual behavior that is affecting job performance can encourage workers to contact a counselor.

After initial medical exams and a counseling session, patients are generally referred to a hospital or outpatient drug clinic for treatment, which may take four to six weeks. During that period, the employees are given sick leave with pay, and their status is kept confidential. Company health-insurance benefits pay all or some of the treatment costs.

Many large companies have made it easier for employees to seek help by setting up nationwide hotlines with toll-free numbers that workers and their families can call to get advice on drug problems. The service offers a guarantee of privacy to employees who are reluctant to approach their bosses or to stop by medical departments.

Employee assistance programs have reduced workplace accident rates by as much as 81%, according to some studies. These programs have also been credited with reducing absenteeism by 80% among participants in several programs.

It's one thing for a large company to set up an in-house program. But for smaller companies there's efficiency as well as safety in numbers by taking a coalition approach to the problem.

At least 300 business leaders in Washington state have embarked on an effort called Washington State Drug Free Business, a statewide group that oversees ten "drug free business initiatives," developing regional support programs for employers.

Businesses in Independence, Missouri are reaping the benefits of a $70,000 grant from the Occupational Safety and Health Administration to the Independence Chamber of Commerce.

In Montgomery County, Maryland, two workplace drug-prevention programs are helping companies sort out their rights and responsibilities in fighting drug abuse among workers. A program set up by the Gaithersburg (Maryland) and Upper Montgomery Chamber of Commerce gives step-by-step instructions in instituting a company drug policy, drug testing, and the benefits of treatment plans like employee-assistance programs. Business Against Drugs Inc., also in Montgomery, is a private-sector group that works closely with the county government to fight drug abuse.

Recommendations on Drug Treatment Programs:

You can find out more about forming a consortium with other businesses by contacting your local Chamber of Commerce. Or you can hire an EAP consultant. Outside of the Yellow Pages you can get the EAP Consultants Directory for $15 from EAPA, (Employee Assistance Professionals Association, Inc.) by writing to them at 4601 N. Fairfax Drive, Suite 1001, Arlington, VA 22203.

The second place to look is at your insurance policy. Visits to a drug treatment center may already be covered. Ask your insurance agent if you're not sure.

According to Susan Berger of the Corporation Against Drug Abuse, "the types of services covered and the lengths of stay allowed vary and are increasingly less generous than in the past."

The *National Institute on Drug Abuse* has a toll-free helpline which refers you to people who can help your company set up a drug education program. It's (800) 843-4971 and the lines are open until 8 p.m., Eastern Standard Time.

Make Your Policies Known

Once you have made a commitment to a drug-free workplace, it's crucial to communicate that commitment to your employees:

- Issue a formal written policy commitment to a drug-free workplace.
- Explain your plans for testing, if any, and the consequences of refusing to be tested and violating your abuse-prevention program.
- Make it clear that law enforcement officials will be contacted regarding the sale, purchase, or possession of illegal drugs on the job.

Communicating your policy should be done through direct briefings, notices in company newsletters, paycheck envelopes, and on bulletin boards and in letters from the company president or plant managers. Your job applications and employee handbooks should carry statements making it clear that employment at your company is contingent on the person being drug-free. Your program should include arrangements for educating employees on the danger of drug abuse.

Keep all possible lines of communication open and recognize the importance of employee suggestions and feedback on the company's program. It's a good idea to designate a contact person with whom employees can discuss drug abuse concerns regarding themselves or fellow workers.

"Local police should know of your program and your willingness to cooperate with them in criminal investigations of illegal drug activity," says the Institute for a Drug-Free Workplace's de Bernardo.

Keep thorough records on test results, accidents and other drug-related incidents. Your best defense against a challenge on disciplinary action is documentation. Keep the records secure and confidential.

For More Information

Publications

Drug Abuse in the Workplace: An Employer's Guide for Prevention, Publication No. 6972, U.S. Chamber of Commerce, 121 pages, $33 for non-members, $20 for members. A guide to establishing policy coordination, communication and enforcement of a worksite drug program. Call (301) 468-5128 or write 1615 H Street NW, Washington, D.C. 20062.

The CADA Guide to a Drug-Free Workplace, 62 pages, $10.60.; *Establishing a Drug-Free Workplace, A Legal Handbook,* 99 pages, $15.90; both by The Corporation Against Drug Abuse. Legal issues to be considered when developing or refining drug policies and programs. Call (202) 338-

0654 or write 1010 Wisconsin Avenue NW, Suite 250, Washington, D.C. 20007.

Quarterly Report on Workplace Issues, The Institute for a Drug-Free Workplace. Call (202) 463-5530 or write P.O. Box 65708, Washington, D.C. 20035-5708.

Guideline for Developing an Employee Assistance Program, James T. Wrich, 1982, 82 pages, $10. Provides detailed implementation procedures, discusses cost factors. Write American Management Association Publications Division, 135 W. 50th St., New York, NY 10020.

Preventing Drug Abuse in the Workplace, Judith Vicary and Henry Resnick, 1982, 53 pages, single copy free. Describes approaches and issues on drug abuse prevention. Write the National Clearinghouse for Drug Abuse Information, P.O. Box 416, Kensington, MD 20795.

Labs That Do Drug Testing

To get a list of the labs certified by NIDA, write to Donna Bush, chief of the drug testing section, Division of Applied Research, National Institute on Drug Abuse, Rockville, MD 20857; (301) 443-6014.

CHAPTER 12
GROUP LIFE INSURANCE

Employer-provided group life insurance is, for many families, the sole source of significant insurance benefits if a worker dies, simply because many people don't buy individual life insurance policies for themselves. This benefit is relatively inexpensive and provides a high degree of security for your employees.

In the insurance business, a benefit that someone is likely to use is going to cost you more than one that isn't likely to be used. Your employees are much more likely to get sick than to die, which is why medical insurance is expensive and life insurance is relatively cheap at most ages. For that reason, many employers pay the whole premium for group life insurance instead of requiring employee contributions.

Employer-provided life insurance is almost always what's called group term insurance. The premiums increase with age, ranging from about 5 cents per $1,000 insurance per month for a female non-smoker in her 20s to more than $1.00 per $1,000 for a male in his 60s. Group rates are generally comparable to the term rates a healthy individual would pay for a single policy through a professional association or directly from an insurance company.

A major advantage of group term products is that less screening is involved than with individual policies, so that people with medical conditions who otherwise couldn't buy coverage on their own may get group coverage. On the other hand, the death benefit is usually small. However, for very small companies, group term life insurance resembles individual term insurance and underwriting via a medical questionnaire may be conducted on each employee.

Under many group life insurance policies, permanent, full-time employees are eligible for coverage on their first day of active employment, unlike other benefits such as long-term disability coverage which require a waiting period. Cash benefits are provided to deceased employees' survivors whether the employees die on or off the job and whether they die from accidental or natural causes. The benefit terminates when employment does (except sometimes in the case of retirees) or shortly thereafter.

This coverage is basically monthly renewable term insurance with rates changing annually, written on a group basis. The cost for term insurance rises with the ages of people insured.

Most medium-to-large companies buy insurance with death benefits of one to two times current annual pay, which is called the earnings or compensation approach to setting life insurance benefits. The problem with this method is that it provides richer benefits to older employees who are closer to retirement and less likely to have dependents who need the protection than it does to younger employees with young children who do.

This is why the "layers of optional benefits" approach is becoming more popular. This is an alternative that gives employees flexibility in tailoring the amount of their group life coverage to their needs and ability to pay. For example, a company might pay for a plan with a death benefit equal to 100% of an employee's annual earnings and have the insurer offer an option for the employee to buy supplemental group term life coverage equal to 200% or 300% of annual earnings at group term rates.

One major life insurer provides additional life insurance amounts in excess of $150,000 to a maximum of $1 million. To get the additional amounts, the employee has to submit medical evidence of insurability.

Another kind of product is a purely voluntary, employee-pay-all insurance. Employees can apply for insurance amounts equal to one, two, or three times earnings.

KEY PERSON LIFE INSURANCE

Key employee life insurance is insurance on a key employee's life owned by the employer, with the death benefit payable to the employer. Technically, key employee insurance isn't an employee benefit; it provides for the continuity of the business in the event of a loss. This is similar to the business protection coverage you would buy in the event of a key person's disability that we described in Chapter Seven.

Businesses buy life insurance on key employees—a partner in the firm, perhaps, or another executive—for three main reasons:

1. To compensate for the loss of earnings caused by the death of a single valued employee.
2. To assure creditors that the business will have extra liquidity to meet its obligations in the event of the death of a key employee.
3. To resolve the ownership of a partnership, a closely held corporation, or a sole proprietorship in the case of the death of one of the owners.

There are various kinds of insurance available for this need and the need for disability insurance for key employees. This is an issue to work out with your accountant and attorney.

TAX AND DISCRIMINATION ISSUES

If you buy more than $50,000 worth of life insurance for an employee, he or she will pay taxes on the value of the extra coverage. Generally, you can deduct the cost of providing life insurance as a business expense.

The Tax Equity and Fiscal Responsibility Act of 1982 (TEFRA) deals with equitable treatment of all employees regarding benefits. The law states that if you give better benefits to a key employee who is either an officer or a major owner, the premium for the first $50,000 of their insurance premium is not deductible. What's more, the cost of the insurance is taxed to the employee.

A key employee is defined as one who within the past four years has been either an officer of the company; one of the ten employees owning the largest interest in the company; a more than 5% owner of the company; or a more than 1% owner of the company who makes more than $150,000 a year.

In order to be non-discriminatory the plan must, for the most part, benefit at least 70% of the employees, and at least 85% of the plan's participants can't be "key employees."

Rules for smaller employees: The IRS requires that companies with fewer than 10 employees can't offer a benefit for employees in a certain income bracket which is more than 2 1/2 times the benefit for the next lower bracket. Also, the coverage in the lowest bracket has to be at least 10% of the amount in the highest bracket. This avoids skewing the benefits to older, more highly compensated employees. And all full-time employees of the company must be covered by the plan.

DEPENDENT GROUP LIFE INSURANCE

Some employers provide group life insurance on the children and spouses of covered employees as well on the employees themselves. Many insurers won't allow an employee to buy dependent group life coverage unless he or she also participates in the basic group plan.

Usually the coverage is not very large. For children, the benefits seem to be designed to cover the cost of funerals. If employees want more coverage, they typically contribute to the cost through a group program or buy coverage on their own.

The insurance laws of many states limit the amount of dependent group life coverage that may be written, so benefit amounts are usually relatively low. What's more, employees will have to pay tax on amounts higher than $2,000 if the coverage is paid for by the employer.

One major life insurer pays a lump sum in amounts of $1,000 up to $5,000 for spouses but not exceeding 50% of the employee's coverage. The company covers children from six months of age to age 23 (25 for fulltime students) for up to $2,500. Children between 14 days and six months old are covered at the rate of 10% of the spouse's coverage.

ACCIDENTAL DEATH AND DISMEMBERMENT

As gruesome as this may sound, accidental death and dismemberment insurance pays a benefit after an accidental death or if a person loses a limb or eyesight from accidental bodily injury—independent of any other cause—within 90 days of the injury.

A typical policy will pay some multiple of salary up to a maximum of $500,000 for the loss of both hands, feet, eyes, or any combination of loss of one hand and one foot and the sight of one eye. It will pay one-half of the amount of basic life insurance for the loss of one hand, foot, or eye.

AD&D doesn't cost as much as life insurance because non-accidental deaths aren't covered. AD&D isn't a substitute for regular life insurance.

GROUP TRAVEL ACCIDENT INSURANCE

This usually covers death or dismemberment due to accidents while employees are traveling on company business. The cost is usually very low and is paid for by the employer. Of course, a company whose employees travel a lot on business should expect to pay more for this coverage than other businesses.

LIFE INSURANCE FOR OLDER WORKERS

The Age Discrimination in Employment Act prohibits discrimination on the basis of age against individuals in the age group between 40 and 70 with respect to terms, conditions, or privileges of employment. Employers are permitted to reduce the benefits provided to older workers if they still spend the same amount on older workers as they do on younger workers. Your insurer should be prepared to meet the rules without any hassle to you.

Generally, benefit experts say companies can reduce the life insurance coverage each year starting at age 65 by 8% of the benefit or make a one-time reduction in life insurance benefits at age 65 by 35% and maintain that reduced amount in force until age 70.

CONVERSION PRIVILEGE FOR TERMINATED EMPLOYEES

Group term life contracts usually contain a provision that allows recently terminated employees to convert part or all of their group life insurance to an individual policy without having to prove insurability. The value of this benefit is that a terminated employee who is uninsurable because of ill health will be able to continue coverage. The employee pays the premium for the converted policy.

This so-called conversion right is mandated by law in some states. The insurance company, rather than the employer, is charged with notifying eligible employees of this right.

DISABLED EX-EMPLOYEES AND DEATH BENEFITS

When an employee becomes totally disabled and stops being an active full-time employee, normally his life insurance coverage would stop 31 days after his termination of employment. But this is the time when he needs life insurance the most. Disabled people usually also have to pay much higher rates for life insurance.

Group term life policies can contain various provisions for continuing coverage under these circumstances. The most common provision is the *waiver-of-premium disability benefit.* Under this provision, the person's life insurance remains in force without further premium payment if the disability started while the person was covered under the group plan. The insurance may continue to age 65.

Some plans require that disability begin before the employee reaches a specified age, such as 60 or 65, although any such requirement is subject to the Age Discrimination in Employment Act discussed earlier in the chapter.

RECOMMENDATIONS FOR BUYING GROUP LIFE COVERAGE:

- If you can afford it, you should buy life insurance for your employees that is two to three times their annual salaries.
- Ask your insurance broker if you can get a "package deal" by buying your life insurance from the same company that sells you your health coverage. Frequently health insurers will *require* small companies to buy life insurance as well, since health coverage is often such an unprofitable product.
- Ask your broker to find an insurer that gives employees the option to buy extra life insurance on a group basis.
- Buy a disability waiver of premium policy so that the life insurance will be continued on disabled employees.
- For the best benefit value, buy group term insurance. Be cautious about *group universal life insurance*, usually an employee-pay-all scheme which allows employees to vary the timing and amount of premiums in addition to the amount of the death benefit and the extent to which it increases.

While group universal life programs may offer lower premiums than individual universal life products, there are these downsides:

- They don't always allow spouse and child coverage.
- The premiums are paid from after-tax dollars.
- There may be changes in the policies if the group contract is terminated.
- There may be a penalty if the policy is surrendered.
- The policies are generally more expensive than group term.

CHAPTER 13
SIMPLE PENSION PLAN OPTIONS

In this chapter we are going to discuss simple pension plans that concentrate on providing a real benefit to employees when they retire. There are a few simple and low-cost ways to set up pension plans; as your business grows, you can adopt a fancier plan.

In keeping with the philosophy of this book, which is to address plans that primarily provide benefits, we are not going to go into detail about the various tax shelters that happen to be called pension plans. We advise those readers with substantial incomes to ask their accountant or attorney about the various ways of sheltering income.

Pension plans are one of the most important benefits a company can provide an employee. Unlike self-employed people, who have ready-made pension plan options from the government—SEP plans, Keoghs, and others—your employees don't have many choices available to them to set up their own retirement plans if you don't have one in place.

In fact, there's only one possibility for employees to put pre-tax dollars into a pension plan on their own: the Individual Retirement Account (IRA). IRAs may be better than nothing, but that's about it. The most an individual can contribute is small: $2,000 per year (slightly higher for someone with a non-working spouse) even if a person is not covered by a plan at work.

Despite the fact that small businesses SHOULD have pension plans for their employees, many of them don't. According to one survey, only 17% of employees in firms with 24 and fewer employees had an employer-based pension plan, and only 44% in firms with 25 to 99 employees did. This compares to 79% of firms with 100 or more employees.

The reasons? Small companies' per capita costs to set up and maintain these plans are a huge multiple of what a large employer would pay because of coping with mind-boggling regulatory requirements. And small companies often have less of a cash cushion than larger companies. Smaller employers may also feel less strongly motivated to set up a pension plan because they have a higher turnover and therefore their employees are less likely to stay at the company long enough to collect a pension.

As pointed out in a 1990 study on pensions and small business for the Small Business Administration, the rules of the game keep changing: 11 major legislative initiatives have changed the regulatory requirements on pensions since the Employee Retirement Income Security Act (ERISA) was passed in 1974. Most of these regulations involve making sure the plan doesn't favor highly compensated employees over the lower-paid and is not being used chiefly as a tax shelter instead of a pension vehicle.

Figure 13-1

SUMMARY OF PENSION PLAN SET-UP AND ADMINISTRATIVE COSTS FOR SMALL AND INTERMEDIATE SIZE PLANS

	Defined Contribution Plans		Defined Benefit Plans	
	25 Participants	*200 Participants*	*25 Participants*	*200 Participants*
SET UP COSTS				
Average Cost Per Plan	$2,018	$4,278	$2,755	$6,117
Cost Per Participant	$81	$21	$100	$31
ANNUAL ADMINISTRATIVE COST				
Average Cost Per Plan	$1,767	$4,997	$2,651	$7,747
Cost Per Participant	$71	$25	$106	$39
REVISIONS AND COMPLIANCE COST				
Average Cost Per Plan	$1,060	$1,755	$1,482	$2,626
Cost Per Participant	$42	$9	$59	$13

SOURCE: Lewin/ICF interviews of pension plan service providers, December 1989.

Just to make things ridiculous, if you make major changes in the provisions of your pension plan, you not only should ask the IRS for permission but you pay a fee as well, ranging from $50 to $1,000. If plans with fewer than 100 employees terminate, the IRS charges $200.

In Figure 13-1 we see some numbers from the SBA study that illustrate how economies of scale make it much more costly per capita for a smaller company to set up a plan. The set-up costs for a defined contribution plan (we'll explain this term later) for a small company are $81 per employee versus $21 for a middle-sized company, and the annual administrative fees run $71 a head versus $25 for middle-sized plans. Defined benefit plans run $110 per participant versus $31 per participant for middle-sized plans.

The complexity and rapid change of the regulations and the high cost of setting up and maintaining a plan can explain in large part why so many small companies have "dropped out" of the pension game. IRS data indicate that since 1982, when new plan formations peaked at 85,000, the rate of new starts has consistently dropped to an estimated 24,700 in 1989.

These data corroborate a study conducted by the National Federation of Independent Business in 1985, which asked employers why they terminated plans once they set them up. Thirty-five percent said they did so because of changing and complex regulations, 25% cited reduced profitability or sales, 8% cited increased administrative costs.

Congress isn't sound asleep at the switch, however. There are federal proposals that would ease the regulatory headache for small business. We'll deal with these ideas in Chapter Sixteen on pension legislation.

PENSION CHOICES

There are fundamentally two kinds of pension plans available. The traditional kind, defined benefit plans, promise employees a set amount when they retire. The second kind, a defined contribution plan, promises to make contributions but doesn't guarantee that those contributions will add up to a set amount.

DEFINED CONTRIBUTION PLAN

Not surprisingly, the defined contribution plan is more popular among smaller companies, because smaller companies have fewer resources available than their larger counterparts to keep the promises that a defined benefit plan makes.

If your aim is to spread enough of your profits around to keep your employees working for you as long as possible, a popular approach is the defined contribution plan. In this setup, you promise your employees that you'll make annual or irregular contributions to their individual accounts—but you won't guarantee that these are going to add up to any particular dollar amount when employees retire. Some varieties of defined contribution plans are really more like "undefined contribution" plans because you don't promise to contribute to them even in good years.

Under the defined contribution setup, the value of the final benefit an employee gets is the total of your contributions, employee contributions if applicable, investment gains or losses, and possibly forfeited unvested employer contributions, which are then parceled out to the accounts of the employees who stay with the company. The investment gains or losses are generally unpredictable, as are some of the other elements, so the final benefit usually can't be predicted very accurately.

We're going to describe four kinds of defined contribution plans in the first part of this chapter: profit-sharing plans, money purchase plans, 401(k) plans, Simplified Employee Pension plans, and IRAs.

Profit-Sharing

The year was 1982. The place was Charlottesville, Virginia and Peter L. Sheeran, the 33-year-old president of Sheeran Cleveland Architects, was fit to be tied. In less than a year, five of his seven full-time architects and designers had jumped ship for larger, more established firms. And he feared the rapid turnover would spell the end of his small, three-year-old professional corporation.

"I knew something had to be done," Sheeran remembers, "but I didn't know what." So he and his partner, Samuel S. Cleveland, sat down and ticked off their options. They could match competitors' offers of better pay. "A financial impossibility," they decided. They could take a crack at stock options. "An administrative nightmare," they figured. Or they could have a go at a profit-sharing plan.

"We wanted," Sheeran says, "to find a way to reward people, so that they knew the harder they worked, the more money they would make. A profit-sharing plan seemed to fit the bill." The first year, Sheeran Cleveland's profit-sharing plan doled out a generous 50% of the firm's earnings to employees. In no time at all, productivity jumped. "People started working nights and coming in early," Sheeran recalls, "and they started taking on more responsibilities without the partners having to delegate to them."

Profit-sharing plans are probably the most appealing plans to small business, if not the most popular. They're ideal when an employer's profits or his ability to contribute varies year to year. In fact, the word "profit" is a misnomer; contributions can be made even if there hasn't been a profit in a given year.

A profit-sharing plan allows a business owner to set aside up to 15% of each employee's annual compensation on a tax-deductible basis. Under this type of plan, the percentages can change each year depending on the company's fortunes. Employees don't have to contribute anything to a profit-sharing plan.

How much to contribute? There are two different ways to determine employer contributions:

- Under a *discretionary* provision, the employer can arbitrarily decide what he or she wants to contribute each year. This is an example of an "undefined" contribution plan. The employer doesn't have to contribute if there is a profit, and can choose to contribute if there isn't a profit. The danger is that if you go too many years without making a contribution, the IRS may decide that the plan is terminated and so all your employees are immediately vested—i.e., employees have the rights to all the money in their accounts.
- Under a *formula* approach, a calculated amount must be contributed to the plan whenever the employer has profits—although you can add a clause to your plan specifying that you don't have to make payments if certain adverse conditions occur. For example, a formula might provide that the employer will contribute 10% of all company profits in excess of $250,000, up to the limits set by tax laws.

How much to contribute per employee? The allocation is usually based on the employee's compensation, with some plans using a flat percentage of salary and others calculating the amount based on the proportion of the employee's compensation relative to the other employee participants. The contributions can also be integrated with Social Security. However, the employer can't deduct any more than 15% of all covered employees' compensation for federal tax purposes. If a company has both a profit-sharing and a money purchase pension plan (explained later in the chapter) covering the same employees, the combined tax deductible contributions can't exceed 25% of all covered employees' compensation.

A profit-sharing plan may include employee contributions in the form of pre-tax salary reduction. If so, it is considered to be a 401(k) plan (also described later), and must follow those rules.

When do employees get their money? There are three different ways of distributing the proceeds of profit-sharing plans:

- Cash plan: Employees get the cash when the profits are distributed, in the form of cash or checks. The amount is taxed as ordinary income when distributed. This is not considered a "qualified" (tax-favored) retirement plan because employees get the money before retirement.
- Deferred: Employees start to get the profit-sharing contributions and investment earnings when they retire or leave the company and begin to pay taxes on the earnings at that point. This seems to be the most popular option, representing 78% of all profit-sharing plans, according to the Department of Labor.
- Combination plan: Just like it sounds—the money is split up between immediate and deferred categories.

Vesting: A key component to the success of profit-sharing plans is to set up a federally approved schedule that determines the percentage of money an employee is entitled to after each year of service, called "vesting" in insurance-ese. Participants become vested in employer contributions after a specified number of years on the job; they are always 100% vested on their own contributions and any earnings on their own contributions.

The trick is to design a schedule that meets the laws and is short enough to appeal to employees but long enough to keep them around as employees. The most common vesting formula in profit-sharing plans is "3-to-7-year," which means the employee isn't vested at all until after three years, when he's 20% vested, increasing an additional 20 percentage points a year until reaching 100% vesting after seven years.

Disadvantages: The retirement benefits may not be adequate for employees who enter the plan at older ages. Employees bear investment risk under the plans.

Recommended: Benefit experts recommend profit-sharing plans for companies who are in cyclical businesses with young employees who have plenty of time to accumulate retirement savings. This is because the contributions are flexible—either discretionary or dependent on the employer's profitability. It's fairly easy to administer.

"I'd recommend it for a startup business that is cyclical with a fair amount of turnover," said Joel Isaacson, a CPA who is director of financial planning for Weber Lipshie & Co. in New York City. "This is for an employer who wants to pass on the rewards of the business in good times but share the burden of bad times as well."

Money Purchase Plan

In a money purchase plan the employer makes annual contributions to each employee's account. It's considered one of the simplest of all plans to administer.

Sound like a profit-sharing plan? Not quite. The formula usually requires a contribution of a specified percentage—up to 25%—of each employee's annual compensation, which is more generous than the 15% limit on profit-sharing plans. Annual employer contributions are required, making it more strict than a profit-sharing plan in which you can skip a year. This is a "real" defined contribution plan.

Tax deductible limits for an employer contribution is adjusted annually for changes in the Consumer Price Index; the limit is the lesser of 25% of compensation or $30,000 in 1991. This amount is reduced by employee contributions and forfeitures from other participant's accounts.

Tax implications: Employer contributions are deductible when made. In certain cases the contribution can be made after the end of a tax year and still be deductible for that year. Both employer contributions and earnings on plan assets aren't taxable to plan participants until they're withdrawn.

Vesting: Any permitted vesting schedule can be used. One version offers no vesting for five years, then 100% vesting after five years of service. This is called "cliff" vesting. Another common vesting schedule is 20% vesting after three years of service, increasing at 20% each year until full vesting is reached after seven years.

Disadvantages for employees: The retirement benefits may not be adequate if they enter the plan at older ages. Employees also bear investment risk under the plans.

Disadvantages for employers: The major disadvantage is that the contributions are required, not optional.

Recommended: When an employer needs simplicity and the employees are relatively young and can afford risk.

401(k) Plan

Easily the most popular of the new defined contribution programs among larger corporations, the 401(k) arrangement permits employees to contribute elective, pretax money to a qualified retirement plan and also allows tax deductible employer contributions. More than 27.5 million workers were covered by these plans in 1988—a nearly 300% increase from the 7.1 million figure five years earlier.

The attraction of 401(k)s to larger businesses is fairly straightforward: it's a heck of a lot cheaper to set up a company pension plan in which the employees have to contribute some or all of the money, as opposed to defined benefit plans in which the employer generally foots the entire bill and bears the investment risk.

The attraction to employees is that a 401(k) (named after the section of the IRS code that brought it into being) looks and quacks almost like an Individual Retirement Account did before the Tax Reform Act of 1986 took away universally tax deductible IRAs. While pre-tax employee contributions for a 401(k) are limited by federal law, the limits—$8,475 in 1991—are much higher than the $2,000 ceiling for an IRA.

Employer contributions are also limited: the sum of all contributions can't exceed the lesser of 25% of an employee's compensation or an amount indexed for inflation, $30,000 in 1991. Employers can either contribute an arbitrary amount, match a certain percentage of employee contributions or allocate a profit-sharing distribution.

In order for 401(k) contributions to be tax deductible, a percentage of employees at all salary levels must participate. So compliance with the non-discrimination rules can be tricky if lower-salaried workers don't bother participating. To motivate contributions from lower-paid staffers, some benefit experts advise matching contributions—say dollar for dollar up to 3% of income versus the typical 50 cents per dollar up to 6% of income—or make a straight-out contribution to each employee's account.

How employee elective contributions work: In the employee contribution arrangement, the employee's salary is reduced and therefore the amount of federal and sometimes state income tax is reduced.

Employees can typically choose which kind of investments their 401(k) contributions should be allocated among, although the choices are generally limited to company-approved investments. For small businesses, these investments are usually chosen by an investment house or brokerage that operates a "turnkey" 401(k) plan. A turnkey plan is one that a variety of companies can use, as opposed to one that is tailor-made to your own business.

Common investment options in a turnkey plan include:

- GICs: guaranteed interest contracts—similar to certificates of deposit but not federally insured—with an insurance company.
- A balanced fund: a mix of stocks and bonds to create safety.
- An equity fund: usually the most risky.
- A money market fund: short-term securities.

Other options include bond funds, fixed income securities, and company stock.

Note: If a brokerage or investment house is administering your 401(k), allowing your employees to direct their own investments will probably cost you or them more money. However, the expense could be well worth it: if an employee-directed investment policy meets Department of Labor standards, there's less likelihood that the employee will be able to blame you (i.e., sue you and win) if the investment performs poorly.

Vesting: Participants are always 100% vested in their own contributions and any earnings on their own contributions, and employer contributions must meet federal vesting standards. Most 401(k)s provide for partial vesting in employer contributions after three years, increasing to 100% after seven years. Forfeited amounts from employees who leave the company before full vesting can be divvied up among the other plan participants and used to reduce future employer contributions.

Advantages to employees: Along with the ability to fund the plans with pre-tax dollars and to choose how the money is invested, one of the features that attracts employees to 401(k)s is that they can get at the money more easily than with other plans, such as IRAs. The 401(k) can be designed so employees can borrow from their accounts—great news if they're looking for a down payment for a house or college tuition for the kids. While most loans from these plans have a five-year payback period, an employee might have as long as 20 years to retire the debt if the loan is used to buy a house.

Advantages to employers:

- As with other pension plans, the employer gets a tax deduction on employer contributions, provided he follows the rules.
- Pressure is reduced to improve other employee benefits.
- 401(k)s are less risky than defined benefit programs because the employer is not guaranteeing a benefit, he is guaranteeing a contribution.

Not recommended: If you're on a tight budget and you're "top heavy" with highly compensated employees.

Only 8% of workers in firms with between ten and 24 workers were covered by 401(k)s as of 1988, says the Employee Benefit Research Institute, compared to 42% in firms with more than 250 employees. Here's why: these plans can require a lot of expensive administrative work to comply with federal non-discrimination rules. These rules are especially tough on partnerships such as law firms or doctors' offices where most of the employees are highly compensated.

Recommended: When an employer can only afford a minimal extra expense beyond existing salary and benefit costs. Many brokerages and financial institutions offer turnkey 401(k) plans and can handle all aspects of setup and administration.

While some pension experts say the company should be made up primarily of young employees who can tolerate risk, Buck Consultants' Fred Rumack contends that "Some plan is better than no plan, even if older employees are involved."

Simplified Employee Pension

Established by the Revenue Act of 1978, the do-it-yourself SEP was supposed to be just what the doctor ordered for gun-shy business owners who employed 25 or fewer people and who couldn't be bothered with the paperwork, complexity and expense of the conventional plans.

But the tax-favored retirement plan still didn't get many takers. It's easy to see why most small businesses don't embrace pensions even when they're simple to administer. When a company is in the startup stage, management is concerned with staying in business long enough to become profitable, as opposed to looking for ways to share those profits with employees.

Because acceptance of pension plans by small business has been slow, Congress has re-designed the SEPs so they won't cost employers much money—by making them "mini-401(k)s" to which the employees are contributing, not just the employers.

Specifically, Congress added a salary reduction feature to the Tax Reform Act of 1986, under which employees can elect to have a portion of their pre-tax salary contributed to a SEP.

We'll deal with the employer-funded variety first:

EMPLOYER-FUNDED SEP

In this arrangement the company establishes an IRA for each eligible employee, who is immediately vested in employer contributions. The limits on SEPs are much higher than on individually-owned IRAs, however—up to the lesser of 15% of compensation, or an amount that will be indexed for inflation: $30,000 in 1991. SEPs can be set up by corporations, unincorporated businesses, partnerships, and self-employed people.

Although employers can choose the investment vehicle, the decision to choose stocks, bonds, mutual funds, or CDs is typically left up to employees, as with 401(k)s.

Employer contributions must be made for each employee who has reached age 21, has worked for the employer during at least three of the preceding five years, even part-time, and has received at least a certain minimum salary from the employer during the year, indexed to inflation (the amount for 1990 was a tiny $342).

Any period of service during the year, even one day, qualifies as work for the year. The employer must contribute for eligible employees who worked some period during the year even if they have left the company by the time the employer makes the contribution.

As you might expect, contributions must be made according to a formula that doesn't discriminate in favor of officers, shareholders, or highly compensated employees. The same percentage of compensation has to be allocated to all eligible employees unless the plans are integrated with social security benefits, in which case you'll need help from a benefits consultant. This kind of help might be worth the extra expense if you wind up spending less money in employee benefit contributions, says benefit expert Joel Isaacson of Weber Lipshie.

The employer then forwards the contributions to the institution managing the IRAs—the bank, insurance company, or mutual fund. The limit on deductible employer contributions is $30,000 per employee, but the total contributions can't be more than 15% of total salaries.

SEPs have the same early-withdrawal penalty as IRAs do: 10% before age 59 1/2. Unlike 401(k) plans, loans can't be made.

Vesting: Employees are 100% vested immediately, even in employer contributions.

Taxation: Employer contributions aren't subject to social security (FICA) taxes or to unemployment taxes.

Here is how to set up the standard IRS model employer-contribution SEP:

- Decide the percentage of pay you want to contribute—it's got to be a uniform percentage for each employee for the standard model.
- Fill out IRS Form 5305-SEP, a quarter page form with six blank spaces.
- Ask your employees to set up IRAs at a financial institution to receive the contributions you make for them.
- Mail the SEP contributions to the financial institution. They can be made up until the date the company's tax return is due.
- Don't file the 5305-SEP with the IRS. Instead, give each employee included in the SEP a completed copy, as well as a statement of the amounts contributed to the employee's SEP accounts.
- There are certain circumstances when the standard IRS model SEP can't be used or where you'll have to seek outside help to tailor the plan to your needs. These are:

  1. If you have another qualified pension plan.
  2. If you have ever had a defined benefit plan.
  3. If you use leased employees.
  4. If the contribution is integrated with social security benefits.

Recommended: for companies with 25 or fewer employees, especially if there isn't a lot of turnover. The fact that contributions can be made up until the employer's tax filing date means that an employer can use a SEP as a temporary measure until a different plan is in place. Tailor-made plans are available from financial institutions, including banks or mutual fund companies.

SALARY REDUCTION SEP

This is the variety of SEP that looks like a 401(k): a salary reduction SEP, which is only available to employees in firms with 25 or fewer employees, at least half of whom must agree to participate.

Employees may elect to defer up to $8,475 in 1991. The limit is reduced by any salary deferral made to a 401(k) arrangement.

"The amount that highly paid employees can contribute before tax may be limited further or totally eliminated if other employees don't contribute or contribute limited amounts," says Fred Rumack of Buck Consultants.

To participate, you use 5305A-SEP form, which isn't filed with your tax return, but distributed to participating employees.

Taxation: Employee elective deferrals are subject to social security (FICA) and unemployment taxes.

A company may have both an employer-funded SEP and a salary reduction SEP, but the total amount contributed per employee can't be more than 15% of pay or $30,000.

Here are commonly asked questions about both kinds of SEPs:

Q: Can an employee who participates in a SEP also contribute to an IRA?

Yes, but the contributions might not be tax-deductible, depending on the employee's income or whether the employee's spouse is already covered by a tax-favored plan.

Q: What if an employee forgets or doesn't bother to set up the IRA?

An employer can set up an IRA at a financial institution on the employee's behalf and make the appropriate contribution.

Advantages of SEPs

- *More flexible contribution arrangements*: Even under the contributory scheme, employers don't have to contribute to SEPs. If a company has a poor year and profits are low, the employer doesn't have to contribute anything. But if you do contribute, you may have to cover everybody who meets the eligibility conditions.
- *More flexible deadlines*: You can open a SEP as late as the tax return filing date for the year in which they are effective, including extensions. Other tax-favored plans have to be adopted before the end of the year in which they are effective.
- *The plans are relatively inexpensive to administer.* Compare these with 401(k) plans, which will run $1,000 or more a year. With a 401(k), the employer has to complete a plan document and will probably need to file with the IRS every time a law changes—and since the law has changed frequently in the last 15 years or so we're talking about a lot of paperwork. With SEPs, on the other hand, there are no plans to file with the Feds; the employer need only furnish the employee with a copy of the executed 5305-SEP or, for salary reduction SEPS, 5305A-SEP.

The disadvantages of SEPs

- *Employers have to pay Social Security taxes on their employees' pre-tax contributions.* And employees would have to pay their portion of Social Security taxes.
- *It's difficult to reward some employees over others through a SEP.* In a non-salary reduction SEP you have to make contributions on behalf of employees who may not remain long with the employer, thus diverting funds you might prefer to use to reward longer-service employees (See Figure 13-2). Because employees vest immediately in employer contributions, employers may feel that such an arrangement doesn't do much to encourage employees to stick around. "If your company has high turnover, SEPs cost you a lot of money," warns Mark Rayford, manager of fund operations at T. Rowe Price.

Figure 13-2

401(K)S VERSUS SALARY REDUCTION SEPS

	SARSEP	*401(k)*
ELIGIBILITY	Age 21. Worked for employer three of last five years. Earns at least $342 this year (1991).	Age 21, one year of service (at least 1,000 hours). Can exclude employees with less than two years of service if employees are fully vested. Can also exclude part-time employees with less than 1,000 hours of service.
MAXIMUM CONTRIBUTION	15% of compensation or $30,000, if less.	15% of compensation or $30,000, if less.
ELECTIVE DEFERRALS	Yes, if following conditions are met: (1) 25 or fewer eligible employees in the preceding year. (2) At least 50% of eligible employees elect a deferral. (3) Maximum of 15% or $8,475 (1991).	Yes. Maximum 15%, or $8,475 (1991).
LIMIT ON ELECTIVE DEFERRALS	Yes. Actual Deferral Percentage (ADP) for each highly compensated employee cannot be more than 125% of ADP for non-highly compensated.	Yes. More complex ADP test is used. Also, average ADP for group of highly compensated is used rather than testing each highly compensated employee, as you would for SEP.
LIFE INSURANCE	Not allowed.	Yes. Must meet incidental test (less than 50% of plan contribution can be used to purchase whole life insurance—25% for universal life).

SOURCE: *Best's Review*, Aug. 1990, p. 40

- *It may be hard to include a relatively low-paid employee in the SEP.* For example, if an employee earns $500 a year and the employer contributes 6% of salary, the employer would have to make a $30 contribution to an IRA. If the employee doesn't have an IRA, some insurance companies or financial institutions may not be willing to accept a $30 investment to set one up.
- *Employees can't make plan loans* or hardship withdrawals as they can with 401(k)s.
- *Salary reduction SEPs won't work if you're too top heavy*: They typically can't be set up by companies that consist only of owners, officers and certain highly-paid employees.

Recommendation: If you're a larger small employer who wants to pick and choose whom you want to cover, you might want to consider a 401(k) instead. If you're smaller you might want to consider sponsoring an IRA since it's easier to administer than a 401(k).

Individual Retirement Account

If you only have a few regular employees but many casual or seasonal employees that you don't want to include in the plan, consider a company-sponsored Individual Retirement Account. IRAs can be made available to any employee or group of employees and not offered to others.

Employers can offer the IRAs through payroll deductions and employees can make investment choices. In contrast with a SEP, each employee with an Individual Retirement Account reports the employer's contribution as income and then takes the normal deduction.

The maximum contribution is $2,000; all or part of it may not be deductible if the employees make too much money and are already covered by a tax-favored plan. Here are the salary limits: The plan is only fully deductible for employees whose adjusted gross income is $25,000 or less filing singly and $40,000 filing jointly. The plans are partially deductible for those with adjusted gross incomes of less than $35,000 filing singly and $50,000 filing jointly.

Recommended: To employers who want to reward certain employees and not others. Only with this approach can the employer pick and choose the recipients.

DEFINED BENEFIT PLAN

A defined benefit plan guarantees a certain level of benefit when the employee retires. For example, a company may promise a benefit equal to 1.5% of an employee's final monthly salary (just before he or she retires) for each year worked.

The danger with this approach is that you're guaranteeing a benefit, and if investment earnings on the pension fund do worse than expected or salaries increase more than expected, you may have to kick in the difference. If your business goes into the doldrums for a while, making required contributions could be tough on you. That's why defined benefit plans tend to be less popular than defined contribution plans among smaller companies, at least those just starting out.

On the other hand, defined benefit plans have been quite popular with very small companies that have been in business for a while, as well as partnerships or professional corporations, in which an older controlling employee wants to maximize tax-deferred retirement savings.

Defined benefit plans can usually take one of three approaches: a flat amount formula, which provides a stated dollar amount to participants; a flat percentage formula, which provides a benefit that's a percentage of the employee's average earnings; and a unit credit formula, which is based on the employee's service with the employer.

Tax implications: There are a host of rules to follow in order for employer contributions to be deductible. Taxation of benefits is deferred until the benefits are withdrawn.

Vesting: The federal minimum vesting standards are the same as for any other qualified plan—either 100% vesting after five years or 20% after three years, increasing by 20% a year to reach 100% after seven years.

There's another problem with defined benefit plans. If Congress decides that your kind of business uses pension plans to dodge taxes (or, the more cynical view, if Congress is simply looking for new places to collect revenue) they could very well sic the IRS on you.

Because some small companies seemed to be deliberately over-funding their pensions in order to lower their tax burden, Congress punished all of them in its 1987 Omnibus Budget Reconciliation Act by lowering the ceiling on allowable contributions, and instructing actuaries to use a higher interest rate to project what their clients' pension investments will earn.

Then in 1990 it went even further, auditing 18,000 small businesses to try to collect $666 million. The IRS particularly scrutinized individual professionals, small law firms, consulting companies, medical practices, and other small firms with highly paid professionals who stashed a lot of money away.

An IRS memo reportedly instructed field agents to deem unacceptable any plans that used interest rate assumptions below 8% or retirement age assumptions under age 65, which were apparently suspicious because they would allow business owners to put more money into the plan than was deemed necessary to fund the retirement package.

"Because of a small number of little guys that did abusive things, (Congress) took out the shotgun," said Craig Miller, president of Westminster USA Ltd. of Scarsdale, New York. "The honest, legitimate guys are finding that the government is no longer being their partner" in providing pensions to employees.

Should you worry about being audited? Not according to Miller. "Actuaries will tend to be more conservative now; we will do what the IRS wants us to do. But we'll warn you that your pension may be underfunded using liberal IRS assumptions and if you want to be more aggressive (in funding the pension), the IRS may disagree with you."

Defined benefit plans are recommended for a business that's been in business for awhile and making lots of money—not for startups. They are ideal for a highly paid owner who is older with younger employees and a fair amount of turnover and can even be used for sole proprietorships (see Keoghs in Chapter Fourteen).

WHY YOU'RE PROBABLY GOING TO NEED HELP SETTING UP YOUR PLAN

There are a huge number of rules for defined contribution plans, as there are for defined benefit plans. We think that reviewing these rules will convince you that you will need professional advice to establish and maintain either of these plans.

Here are some examples of areas where you'll need help:

- Setting the contributions to each employee's account so that the plan isn't discriminatory—or knowing what rules to follow if it is.
- Knowing the rules and penalties regarding withdrawals and loans from the plan, when applicable.
- Figuring out how to distribute the pension benefit once the individual retires: whether in a lump sum or an annuity. Retirees may also be entitled to stretch their tax obligation over a five- or ten-year period. There are also special rules to observe when the employee dies or takes early retirement and there are special rules for married employees.
- Knowing the limit on tax deductible contributions to the particular plan in a given year as they apply to employer and employee.
- Knowing how to integrate plans with the social security benefits—benefits for which you're also making a contribution.
- Knowing when to file statements, changes in the plan with the IRS or Department of Labor.

WHO MANAGES PENSION PLANS

Who do you call to help you set up a pension plan? For the simplest plan, such as the SEP explained earlier in this chapter, you can ask your CPA for help.

For more complicated plans, such as defined benefit plans or 401(k)s, you have two choices. The more traditional "unbundled" method (in which you have greater freedom of choice on investments) involves a fair amount of hiring: You'll need an actuary or administrator to establish the plan and handle record-keeping. You'll also need an investment manager. Unfortunately, many managers have account minimums of $500,000. Independent administrators usually charge by the hour, ranging from $55 to $200. A

401(k) for 100 participants might cost $6,000 to $10,000 a year in administrative fees.

Along with somebody to manage your pension investment, you'll need to hire an actuary if you have a defined benefit plan. This is a person who calculates how much to put in each year to achieve the benefit and tax deductions desired and will take care of the filings. You will also need legal and accounting advice. In addition, you'll need to set up a tax-exempt trust to hold the money.

The other approach, which runs about 30% cheaper, is a turnkey plan, usually offered by a mutual fund company. Here the sponsor does everything: draws up a plan (often a standardized "prototype" plan), handles the administration and government filings, and invests the assets. In turnkey plans, there's usually a flat record-keeping charge of about $500 to $1,000 annually and a fee per participant, which can range from $10 to $55 a head. Fees decrease as enrollment goes up. Fees increase if employees are allowed to switch funds frequently.

The drawbacks: Turnkey plans almost always invest in the sponsor's products, so they can't accommodate a specific investment option, like buying your company's stock. Turnkey plans also may not be flexible enough to accommodate your financial needs. Finally, some turnkey sponsors may not have the skills or commitment to administer your pension over the long haul.

CHAPTER 14

SELF-EMPLOYED PEOPLE

In this chapter we discuss employee benefits for those small companies that have only one employee. In other words, self-employed people. While much of the material on employee benefits in the earlier chapters applies to the self-employed, there are special problems and coverages unique to "groups of size one," as these folks are sometimes described by the insurance industry.

HEALTH BENEFITS

In the four years after the Baltimore News American printed its final edition, laid-off photographer John Davis joined three separate medical insurance plans—and fled each one after skyrocketing premiums drained his family savings.

His fourth plan was no bargain either; he pays a hefty $1,000 a year to cover 80% of his family's medical expenses. And that coverage would only start AFTER he and his family spend $10,000 of their own money first. That's some deductible!

We hate to say this, but the cost of buying health insurance alone is a good reason why you might want to reconsider taking the plunge to become self-employed in the first place—unless those of you who are striking out on your own can get coverage under your spouse's employer's plan. Insurers will consider you a high risk for a host of reasons. There are no other healthy employees in your "company" to counterbalance the fact that you might be a bad risk; there's a good chance you could go broke and stop paying the premiums; and—let's face it—insurance companies may suspect that you're deliberately buying the insurance because you're ill in the first place.

You've already made the decision to go it on your own? There is some good news. If you've recently left a job where you did have health insurance, you can buy coverage at group rates for a while. A federal law called the Consolidated Omnibus Budget Reconciliation Act of 1985 gives you the option to hold onto your old group coverage for 18 months or more as long as you worked for a company with at least 20 employees.

This has two advantages: You'll pay close to the group rate (by law, 102% of it) and your insurer has to keep you regardless of your health history. You may also be able to buy an individual policy from the same insurer that provided the group coverage—although the rates aren't necessarily going to be cheap and coverage probably won't be as comprehensive.

And that brings us to the bad news: the rates. Once you start shopping for coverage, you'll be disappointed to find that even the alternatives you might have thought would be less costly—for example, Blue Cross plans which, in many states, have to insure you, or plans like HMOs—are very costly. For example, one HMO in the Maryland area charged a family of three $4,944 a year. A Blue Cross/Blue Shield plan in the area charged $2,100 a year for coverage with a $500 deductible and copayments that are capped at $2,000, meaning a potential total annual cost of $4,600.

Other possibilities: Your trade association, union, or alumni association may offer "group" health insurance. Be prepared for hefty premiums and substantial deductibles and copayments.

DISABILITY COVERAGE

In August 1979, Ray Porter Jr. was taking the down escalator in the Pan American building in Manhattan, on his way to sell insurance to a client, when he was knocked over by somebody in a hurry to catch a train.

When the 54-year-old New Rochelle native regained consciousness, he was in a hospital packed in ice to control a raging fever. Spinal cord damage had left him almost completely paralyzed—"All I could move was my thumb."

After 11 months of hospitalization, hours of physical therapy, and a strong dose of spunk, Porter wound up walking again. But he never worked again. He moved to Florida and let his staff run his office without him. "Luckily I had a good staff."

How did he pay the medical bills? Because Porter was on his way to a work-related appointment, his company's workers' compensation insurance took care of him, including his medical tab: "over half a million dollars, nearly $1 million."

But if Porter's accident hadn't been on the job, his financial hardship would have been much greater. Despite the fact that Porter managed an insurance agency for a living, he forgot to sell himself insurance to replace his income, better known as disability coverage.

"I said the hell with it. I had four kids. You need life insurance, you need insurance on your car, on your house and by the time you pay for all of that you run out of disposable income."

Porter probably should have known better, but he's in good company. Despite the fact that the average 40-year-old is four times more likely to become disabled than to die, only 30% of the population carries insurance to replace their incomes.

Don't assume that the only reason you'd become disabled is because of a freak accident, either. Dr. Robert Hollomand, a Los Angeles dentist, always prided himself on being in good health. But after years of standing stooped over his patients, his spine gradually deteriorated and ultimately caused him such pain that he couldn't practice dentistry.

"It was a shock to be totally disabled," said Hollomand, who didn't work at all for two months and was not able to resume a full work load for more than six months. Luckily, his disability insurance provided that he would receive a check for $1,400 a month to replace a portion of his lost income.

Paul McAvoy, a financial planner with Westchester Financial Advisory Services in White Plains, New York, insists that disability coverage is even more vital than life insurance. "If you own an oil well, you have that thing insured. That's the way you should treat your own body," says McAvoy.

Many people mistakenly think that social security covers them. But the Social Security Administration's disability criteria are so strict that only about 35% of people who apply for the benefits qualify.

Disability insurance replaces a portion of your income—say, 60% to 70%—in the event you become disabled. Self-employed people need this coverage for two reasons: to keep paying their household bills in the event they are unable to work, and to meet business expenses as well.

Life insurance companies do sell disability coverage to "groups" as small as one person. In practice, these may be individual disability policies. As we mentioned in Chapter Seven, there are also professional overhead expense policies for sole proprietors that pay expenses in the event of a disability.

While disability coverage is often more costly than life insurance, there are ways to cut costs.

- You can extend the waiting period before the coverage kicks in to 180 days instead of 90 days. Of course, this means you will need your own financial resources for those additional 90 days.
- You can buy the coverage while you're young. For example, somebody looking for $3,000 a month in coverage could pay at least $400 a year less if he bought it at age 30 than at age 45.
- Shop for the best price by going to an independent agent or broker.

At the same time, it's also worth it to pay a bit more for coverage that protects your dignity. For example, it's important to get a policy that defines disability as the inability to do the job you used to do, not just any old job. Some policies will virtually consider you fit to work if you can be propped up on a street corner to sell pencils.

Under the most generous definition, known as "own occ" (own occupation), insurers agree to pay full benefits if you can't work in your own occupation as long as you are under a physician's care. In contrast, a policy using the narrower "any occ" definition would pay only if you are unable to work in any occupation for which you are clearly suited.

Insurers commonly compromise by "splitting" the definition of disability and paying benefits under own-occ rules for the first one to five years of a disability and under any-occ rules thereafter. Not surprisingly, pure own-occ policies are 5% to 15% more expensive.

Most experts recommend that you choose a policy that stops paying benefits at age 65, because pension and social security retirement benefits kick in at that age. For premiums about 20% higher, you can select a benefit period that continues until you die. Such a policy would make sense if you are young and there is a possibility that a long term disability would prevent you from building retirement benefits.

As with other products, insurers tend to offer lots of options. A valuable option is the zero-day residual benefit. This option supplements your income if you are well enough to work but not full-time.

Other Pointers

Pick a plan that permits you to add coverage later, no matter what your state of health.

Consider getting a rider that replaces social security benefits in the event you don't qualify for them under the Social Security Administration's strict definition of disability. Some policies offer this benefit as part of the basic policy.

Consider a rider that adjusts your benefits with inflation. There are usually limits to the adjustments, both per year (such as 5% a year) and in total, such as a 100% maximum increase in coverage. For more information on disability insurance, please see Chapter Seven.

RETIREMENT PLANS

Keoghs

During the 1970s and 1980s, the federal government provided tax incentives for self-employed individuals to encourage Keogh plans. Despite these incentives, Keogh plans haven't been hugely popular.

In 1987, 5.6% of some 10 million self-employed people contributed to a Keogh plan, compared with 4.8% of the 9 million self-employed in 1983—not much of an increase, given the fact that the self-employed should have flooded to them after the 1986 Tax Reform Act emasculated the IRA for high wage earners.

Basically a Keogh has the same ceilings for contributions as other corporate pension plans—and the same tax advantages.

To qualify, you can either be a sole proprietor or a member of a partnership, but you can't be incorporated.

Just as with an IRA, there is a full range of investment choices. Banks, mutual fund companies, brokers and life insurance companies sponsor Keoghs.

Keoghs can also be ideal for someone who is in the lucky position of earning so much money he needs to find a tax shelter for it; for example, someone who has self-employment income as well as income from a regular job, and wants to invest as much as possible of the self-employment income to postpone paying taxes on it.

If in the future you stop being self-employed and decide to work for another company, the proceeds can be rolled over to a tax-favored plan with your employer or to an IRA. Uncle Sam just wants to make sure that if you take your money out, you put it into another qualified plan.

If you become totally disabled, you can get at your money without being subject to the premature withdrawal penalty of 10% typically levied against people under age 59 1/2 who withdraw money from their plans.

There are both defined contribution and defined benefit Keoghs: You can invest a limited percentage of your earnings each year in a Keogh structured as a defined contribution plan. Or you can stash away much more money in the defined benefit plan.

Defined Contribution Keoghs

Profit-sharing: a plan that permits you to contribute up to 15% of the net payroll of plan participants—or nothing at all if you've had a bad year. However, the IRS requires you to put in "substantial and recurring contributions" or the plan will be deemed terminated.

Money-purchase plan. It gives you the most mileage by letting you set the annual contribution at a fixed rate as high as 25% of your net income. However, you have to stick to this percentage no matter how prosperous or unprosperous your business is.

Combination plan. This enables you to make maximum contributions without committing yourself to them every year. You can open two accounts, a profit-sharing and a money-purchase plan.

Defined Benefit Keoghs

This is the option in which you guarantee yourself a certain retirement kitty, as we outlined in Chapter Thirteen. These are ideal for those people who are close to retirement age and need to stash away a big chunk of income each year to build up a sufficient nest-egg. You can shelter as much as you want, up to 100% of self-employment income to pay a benefit of as much as $103,000 a year in 1990 dollars. This is a pension plan for people with lots of surplus income.

The downside to a defined benefit approach:

- Defined benefit Keoghs require expensive legal and actuarial help in contrast to simpler profit-sharing and money-purchase plans.
- Defined benefit Keogh plan owners with more than $25,000 in the plan or more than one participant other than a spouse must file a special tax form with the IRS on or before July 31 each year. This filing will require professional help.

Recommended: for people who have lots of excess income to shelter.

SEPs for the Self-Employed

If a Keogh is too unwieldy, consider a Simplified Employee Pension, a do-it-yourself pension that lets you defer federal and state taxes on the income until you withdraw it at retirement time.

While the contribution limits may be lower with a Simplified Employee Pension—up to 15% of net self-employment income or $30,000, whichever is less—they're a lot easier to administer.

"I'd recommend a SEP to anyone who is self-employed and doesn't have any employees, says Steven Enright, a financial planner in Westwood, New Jersey. "It's cleaner and easier to administer." If more money needs to be added after reaching the 15% SEP IRA limit, a Keogh can be added.

With SEPs, the statements are similar to the forms used for an ordinary IRA and the contributions are simply noted on the form. On the other hand, Keogh participants have to send in a special form to the IRS every July.

Downside: The salary reduction SEP, described in greater detail in our chapter on pensions, generally can't be used by companies consisting only of owners, officers or people who otherwise fit the definition of "highly-paid employees."

Advantages of a SEP: You basically set up an IRA for yourself, except that you get to contribute more and deduct more. For more information on SEPs, see the section on them in Chapter Thirteen.

Life Insurance

There are two reasons to buy life insurance as a self-employed person: to help support your family and to help your business pay its bills if you die.

While your insurance agent may try to convince you to buy life insurance coverage that lasts a lifetime or that features an investment component—also called "cash value"—we think the most economical benefit is usually a plain-vanilla term policy. Term insurance provides coverage for a specific period of time, usually as long as you have dependents who rely on your income.

Life insurance products that feature a cash value or investment component are, in the short term, usually more expensive than term policies. These policies, which include whole life, universal life and variable life policies, may offer certain tax advantages on their investment component. But for individuals who are seeking economical death benefits and who don't have a lot of money to shelter from taxes, we recommend term insurance.

We do recommend the disability waiver of premium rider if you don't have disability insurance. This coverage will pay your life insurance premiums if you should become disabled. On the other hand, we think you should stay away from the accidental death benefit rider, which pays survivors double or triple the face amount of the policy if they die in an accident. This is a waste of money, since your death benefit needs aren't larger if you die in an accident than from another cause. What's more, the likelihood of your dying in an accident is small; only about 6% of policyholders are killed in accidents.

CHAPTER 15

HIRING YOUR FIRST EMPLOYEES

You've been successfully self-employed for a year or two. Your phone is ringing off the hook, your appointment calendar is chock-full—in fact, you're so deluged with orders for your product that you're not sure you can continue to handle the workload by yourself.

Congratulations! This is a "dilemma" that most startup businesses hope to confront in the early stages of growth and a strong indicator that your business is going to be a winner.

At this juncture you're faced with a choice: you could turn down the work—and risk losing business to a competitor. Or you could hire extra help. But suppose you're not sure how long your "overload" status is going to last. You'd hate to go to the trouble of employing somebody only to have to hand that person a pink slip in a few months should business start to slump.

OPTIONS

You have a few options. Instead of hiring someone outright, you might consider paying a freelancer a per-project fee—perhaps based on a percentage of the profits of the job. One source of freelancers is local colleges, who often have lists of talented students who need to earn extra money but don't qualify to receive financial aid.

You might also consider "hiring" a temp. A temporary personnel service hires people as its own employees and "rents" them to companies such as yours who need short-term assistance. This means that you aren't hiring employees, you're buying the use of their time.

In this arrangement you don't have to worry about handling bookkeeping headaches such as payroll, tax deductions, workers' compensation insurance, fringe benefits, and other costs connected with the employee —although, of course, you pay the temp service to be relieved of this headache. Nor are you saddled with the obligation to report the individual's withholding and social security taxes and unemployment compensation. Finally, you're relieved of the burden of recruiting, interviewing, screening, and even testing and training the person.

Typically, a temp could be a typist, a secretary, a word processing operator, a bookkeeper, a switchboard operator, a packer, or a salesperson, although there are also professional temps who work as engineers, lawyers, accountants—even chief executives.

Before you "hire" a temp, check out the credentials of the temp firm. Is the company well-established in the field? How many years has it been in business? Does it screen its applicants and check their references? Does the firm make an effort to touch base with you after the assignment is completed to make sure you were satisfied with the temp's performance?

When shouldn't you hire a temp? If you need extra help for longer than six months or if the task is so complex you have to train the temp to do it, it's probably more cost-effective to hire someone outright.

ESTABLISHING JOB DESCRIPTION AND SALARY

Once you make the decision to hire someone for the first time—transforming your status from "self-employed person" to "employer"—you're confronted with a host of duties. For one thing, before you hang a "help wanted" shingle on the door or advertise for help in the want ads, you're going to have to define what kind of help you want.

Here are the factors to consider in developing a job description:

- What responsibilities does the job entail?
- What educational background is necessary to do the job well?
- How many years of experience does the job require, or is it an entry-level one? Is knowledge of certain machinery or computer proficiency required? If so, with what kind of software and hardware should the applicant be familiar?

Next, check your balance sheet and discuss with your accountant how much you can budget for wages and taxes. Then you've got to sit down and figure out what the job is worth. The salary you offer will depend on the job and the going rate.

Contact your state's department of labor or your local office of the U.S. Employment Service for minimum wage requirements, as well as contract and wage stipulations, should you have to deal with a union. You may want to refer to the regional job averages produced by the Bureau of Labor Statistics; selected job categories are listed at the end of this chapter. Talk to other business owners or members of your trade association for further guidelines on salary. Easiest yet, peruse the want ads in your local paper to find out what other employers are paying for jobs with similar levels of skill, experience, responsibility, and education.

How do you develop a formula for figuring compensation? Consider the following factors:

- Higher pay should be given for work requiring more knowledge, skill, or physical exertion.
- Pay should be competitive with that received for similar work in other companies of similar size.
- The salary should reflect the employee's contribution to the performance of the company.

"You Can't Get Good Help Anymore"—or Can You?

Here's the toughest challenge of all: winnowing the field of job candidates down to the one who will be an ideal fit for your growing company. You are going to have to do some detective work to differentiate between a job candidate who is a hardworking team player from one who may offer more style than substance.

Studies show that up to 25 percent of all job applicants fudge the truth when describing their employment credentials. As recruiter Robert Half puts it, "A resume is a balance sheet without any liabilities."

To make matters worse, it's frequently difficult to get an accurate assessment of a prospective worker through references from previous employers because of fears of generating lawsuits from the aggrieved former employee. "A growing number of employees are suing ex-bosses who give them negative references, charging defamation of character," explains Michael Lonto, managing partner of the San Francisco office of Jackson, Lewis Schnitzler & Krupman, a national labor and employment law firm.

For example, a judge ordered one employer to fork over $200,000 in damages for giving this seemingly innocuous reference about a salesperson: "(The employee) was fired for failure to increase business as a major product sales representative."

Therefore, it's very likely that if your prospective employee's job record is tarnished, previous employers won't come out and say so. They may very well restrict the discussion to confirming the period of employment and the salary earned.

So it's up to you to learn how to read between the lines, as well as do your own legwork. For example, you should verify the candidate's college degree by contacting the college itself. When you contact a former employer, you might want to confirm the portion of the job candidate's resume that deals with job duties to make sure that he or she isn't gilding the lily. Then ask the reference for the names of other people to call for information on the candidate, to help obtain a truly objective view of the candidate's strengths or weaknesses.

Once you schedule the job interview, allow at least two hours to up to a full day—depending on the status of the job—for you and the candidate to get to know each other. Prepare for the interview; study the candidate's resume in advance of your face-to-face meeting so that you can jot down further questions. Whenever possible, obtain samples of his or her work.

During the interview, describe the job thoroughly to the job candidate, identifying the duties as specifically as possible. Describe the perks and benefits—as well as the downsides: long hours, for example. Let's face it, if you expect candor from a job candidate you should be candid about the job; you're only cheating yourself if you soft-pedal the negatives and your newly-hired worker winds up quitting.

Then ask the candidate key questions about his or her job experience that would indicate competence or lack thereof. Ask questions that are designed to elicit more than a "yes" or "no" answer. In doing so you can simultaneously measure his or her enthusiasm and skills—or potential attitude problems.

These questions might include:

- What sorts of tasks do you dislike performing?
- What frustrated you the most about your last job?
- What was the toughest situation you had to handle, and how did you handle it?
- Do you prefer to work for a boss who is a delegator or one who gives you full instructions and close supervision?

Have the job applicant sign a release stating that any false information he or she gives you could result in termination. If the job candidate is a high-salaried professional—especially one you'd be entrusting with large sums of cash—it might be worthwhile to invest in the services of a professional reference checker such as Equifax Services in Atlanta or Fidelifacts in New York City.

LAWS THAT AFFECT HIRING, OR WHEN TO BITE YOUR TONGUE

At the same time you'll be questioning the applicant closely about his or her ability to do the work, you don't want to ask personal questions that might be interpreted as violating laws against discrimination.

Here are examples of questions *not* to ask because they may violate a federal law:

1. Don't ask women applicants if they have children, plan to have children, or have child care. You could be violating Title VII of the Civil Rights Act of 1964, which bans discrimination based on race, color, religion, national origin, or sex.
2. Don't ask the applicant's age. The Age Discrimination in Employment Act outlaws discrimination against those aged 40 and above for an employer of a certain size (see below).
3. Don't ask applicants if they have a disability that would prohibit them from carrying out certain tasks. As we mentioned in Chapter Nine, the Americans with Disabilities Act prohibits asking this kind of question of a job candidate before an offer of employment is made.
4. Don't even ask about height or weight on the job application. Obesity can conceivably be considered a protected disability under the disabilities law.

The following is a sampling of the most important federal laws pertaining to fair treatment of employees and job candidates. Most small employers should be familiar with all of these laws. (You may also have to abide by state laws pertaining to employment that are stricter than the applicable federal laws.)

The *Equal Pay Act* prohibits employers from discriminating against employees on the basis of sex by paying lower wages to employees of one sex if the employees work in the same establishment on jobs that require equal skill, effort, and responsibility and are performed under similar working conditions.

The *Fair Labor Standards Act* requires that employees be paid at least the minimum wage and that in general they be paid time-and-one-half for hours worked in excess of 40 in a work week. The law also sets overtime, record-keeping, and child labor standards and covers both full-time and part-time employees.

The *Pregnancy Discrimination Act of 1978* prohibits termination or refusal to hire or promote a woman solely because she is pregnant. It also bars mandatory leaves of absence for pregnant women that are arbitrarily set at a certain time in their pregnancy.

The *Family and Medical Leave Act*, signed into law by President Clinton in February 1993, requires businesses with fifty or more employees to offer all but their top employees up to twelve weeks of unpaid leave per year to take care of a new baby or an ill family member. It also requires employers to maintain health benefits for the employee, and to give the returning employee his/her old job back or one with equivalent pay and benefits. Employers can deny leave to the highest-paid 10 percent of workers if their absence would cause grievous economic harm to the business.

The *Immigration Reform and Control Act* prohibits employers with more than three employees from discriminating by recruiting, hiring, or discharging employees on the basis of national origin, citizenship, or intention to obtain citizenship.

Title VII of the Civil Rights Act of 1964 prohibits employers with 15 or more employees from job discrimination on the basis of race, color, religion, gender, creed, veteran's status, or national origin.

The *Age Discrimination in Employment Act* prohibits employers of 20 or more people from arbitrary age discrimination against people aged 40 and above in hiring, discharge, leave, compensation, and promotion and other matters of employment.

Breaking the News

When you've finished interviewing the job candidate, let the person know when you'll be making your decision. Don't hire anyone on the spot. Take time to mull over each candidate's qualifications.

Once you decide which candidate to hire and the individual has accepted your offer, be gentle when breaking the bad news to the unsuccessful candidates. Write or call them as soon as you make your decision, letting them know that while another candidate was selected for the job, you appreciate their interest and wish them well in their job search.

If you would consider hiring any of the unsuccessful candidates for a similar position in the future, say so. Don't risk alienating individuals who may very well be future job candidates—or customers—by telling them their skills didn't measure up or otherwise comparing them negatively with other candidates.

EMPLOYMENT TAXES

If you think the wages you must pay to attract good people are high these days, wait until you start tallying up the contributions you and your employees must shell out to support them when they're not working—as well as supporting Uncle Sam in the style to which he's become accustomed.

Mandatory costs such as Social Security, unemployment insurance, and workers' compensation insurance add a hefty sum to your payroll costs; an average of almost 9 percent of payroll, according to a survey by the U.S. Chamber of Commerce. What's more, the cost of time not worked, including vacations, holidays, and sick days, amounts to about 11 percent. The costs of providing company-paid benefits such as health insurance and pension plans add another 16 percent. So the total hidden costs of hiring an individual average nearly 36 percent of your payroll costs, not counting the costs of record-keeping. To put it another way, somebody with a weekly gross pay of $400 a week will, on average, cost an employer about $544.

FORMS, FORMS, AND MORE FORMS

Here are some general procedures to observe when becoming an employer. These rules apply to most employers; there are sometimes exceptions for farmers and those employing household workers.

Every business with at least one employee is required to withhold federal income taxes and Social Security taxes. Your first step should be to obtain a federal employer identification number by filing Form SS-4 with your local IRS service center. A federal tax deposit coupon book will be sent to you after you apply for an employer identification number.

The IRS will send you a copy of Circular E, the IRS's Employer's Tax Guide, which indicates the up-to-date amount to withhold from an employee's salary based on the total salary amount. The tax tables will show to the penny how much federal income tax to withhold for single or married people earning a daily, weekly, biweekly, semimonthly, or monthly salary.

(As long as you're picking up forms, stop at your local office of the Immigration and Naturalization Service. Your new employee will also have to fill out Form I-9, which verifies that he or she is either a U.S. citizen or authorized to work in the United States, to comply with the Immigration Reform and Control Act. There are substantial penalties for not completing this form.)

But before you can do any figuring, your employees must tell you how many exemptions they're claiming. They do this by filling out Form W-4, the Employee's Withholding Allowance Certificate. This form must be filled out by every employee—not just new hires—at the beginning of each calendar year. What's more, if an employee gets married, has a baby, or otherwise adds to or subtracts from the number of dependents, a new W-4 should be filled out.

Income tax: Once the W-4 is filled out, you can figure out an employee's withholding tax by using Circular E, as well as taxes for Social Security and Medicare. For tax purposes, wages also include tips, bonuses, and commissions. In most cases, you can simply consult the section of the table that corresponds to the worker's wages and withholding allowance to find out how much must be withheld.

Social Security and Medicare taxes: Now you're ready to calculate how much you and your employee owe the Feds to help pay the employee's living and medical expenses during his or her retirement years. You as an employer must collect and pay the employee's part of the tax and you must pay a matching amount.

The tax rate for Social Security is 6.2 percent each for employers and employees—12.4 percent total—on the first $57,600 of income as of 1993. The tax rate for Medicare is 1.45% each for employers and employees—2.9 percent total—on the first $135,000 as of 1993. There are also tables in Circular E to help you do the calculating.

Paying the taxes: How frequently you pay the taxes depends on how much you owe. Here are the two most common scenarios for small businesses:

- If the total taxes including Social Security and Medicare for all employees are less than $500 in any quarter, you pay the money directly to the IRS using Form 941.
- If the amount is $500 or more in a quarter but less than $50,000 in the previous July 1-through-June 30 period, you deposit the money monthly in an "authorized" bank—most commercial banks qualify—within 15 days after the close of the month and the bank will pay it for you. (More than likely, the bank won't agree to perform this service unless you have an account there.) The IRS will notify you in November if you fall into this category.

Use Form 8109, Federal Tax Deposit Coupon, to deposit employment taxes. You make the check payable to the bank, noting your employer identification number, the type of tax, and the tax period to which it applies, on the check.

Filing your quarterly return: Most employers have to file Form 941 quarterly. This is a summary of the wages and income, Social Security, and Medicare taxes paid during the quarter. It's due by the end of the month following the end of the quarter.

Federal Unemployment Tax: The Federal Unemployment Tax (FUTA), together with your state unemployment tax, provides for payments of unemployment compensation to workers who have lost their jobs.

For 1993, the FUTA tax is 6.2 percent of wages paid during the year on the first $7,000 of wages. Generally you can take a credit against your

FUTA for amounts you paid into your state unemployment fund (see below) up to 5.4 percent of taxable wages.

How to pay FUTA: You use Form 940 or 940 EZ to pay the taxes. You will probably qualify to use the "EZ" form if you paid state unemployment taxes to only one state and you paid them on time. If you owe more than $100 in FUTA by the end of any calendar quarter, you have to deposit it by the end of the following month in an authorized bank.

State unemployment taxes: You also must register with your state's Department of Labor to pay your state unemployment tax. As with the Feds, they will assign you an identification number. How frequently you pay the tax—monthly, quarterly, or annually—will depend on the amount of tax you pay.

State and municipal income taxes: Check with your state Department of Labor to find out the formula for withholding state taxes from your employee paychecks. Again, how frequently you file will depend on the amount of tax you pay. Depending on the size of the metropolis where you do business, you may have to pay a municipal income tax, too.

W-2: You must furnish W-2 forms to all employees by January 31, so they'll have a summary of the previous year's wages and Social Security, Medicare, and withholding taxes.

W-3: These are otherwise known as the Transmittal of Income and Tax Statements. This is the big picture: how much in wages you paid and taxes you withheld for all the employees in your company for the previous calendar year. This goes to the Social Security Administration.

Record-keeping: The Internal Revenue Service says you should keep all records of employment taxes for four years. Keep on hand:

- Your employee identification number.
- Each employee's name, address, and Social Security number.
- The amount and date of salary payments subject to withholding taxes and the amounts withheld.
- The periods of employment, including payments to employees during their absence owing to illness and injury.
- W-4 forms.
- Copies of tax returns that must be filed.

The good news: Does all this bookkeeping, record-keeping, and reconciling sound like the makings of a major migraine? Well, with any luck your business will be sufficiently in the black that you'll be able to afford to hire a payroll service to handle the responsibility. For as little as $30 to $60 a month, such services can handle all of these tasks, as well as taking care of your year-end payroll tax work. Good luck!

Figure 15-1

NATIONAL AVERAGE HOURLY EARNINGS OF PRODUCTION OR NONSUPERVISORY WORKERS ON PRIVATE NONFARM PAYROLLS, BY SELECTED INDUSTRY (AUGUST 1992)* (NOT SEASONALLY ADJUSTED)

Industry	1987 SIC Code	Average hourly earnings
		August 1992
TOTAL PRIVATE		$10.56
MINING		14.45
Oil and gas extraction	13	13.92
Crude petroleum and natural gas	131	16.62
Oil and gas field services	138	12.23
CONSTRUCTION		14.20
General building contractors	15	13.49
Residential building construction	152	12.65
Operative builders	153	13.82
Nonresidential building construction	154	14.27
Special trade contractors	17	14.46
Plumbing, heating, and air conditioning	171	14.82
Painting and paper hanging	172	13.25
Electrical work	173	15.41
Masonry, stonework, and plastering	174	14.58
Carpentry and floor work	175	14.57
Roofing, siding, and sheet metal work	176	12.71
MANUFACTURING		11.44
DURABLE GOODS		12.04
Lumber and wood products	24	9.49
Logging	241	11.36
Sawmills and planing mills	242	9.63
Sawmills and planing mills, general	2421	9.99
Hardwood dimension and flooring mills	2426	7.99
Millwork, plywood, and structural members	243	9.53
Millwork	2431	9.85
Wood kitchen cabinets	2434	8.90
Hardwood veneer and plywood	2435	8.21
Softwood veneer and plywood	2436	11.12
Wood containers	244	6.92
Wood buildings and mobile homes	245	9.22
Mobile homes	2451	9.27
Miscellaneous wood products	249	8.73
Furniture and fixtures	25	9.04
Household furniture	251	8.44
Wood household furniture	2511	7.88
Upholstered household furniture	2512	9.22
Metal household furniture	2514	8.46
Mattresses and bedsprings	2515	8.82
Office furniture	252	9.74
Public building and related furniture	253	9.45
Partitions and fixtures	254	10.43

*Source: *Employment and Earnings*, U.S. Department of Labor, November 1992.

NATIONAL AVERAGE HOURLY EARNINGS OF PRODUCTION OR NONSUPERVISORY WORKERS ON PRIVATE NONFARM PAYROLLS, BY SELECTED INDUSTRY (AUGUST 1992)—CONTINUED (NOT SEASONALLY ADJUSTED)

Industry	1987 SIC Code	Average hourly earnings
		August 1992
DURABLE GOODS—CONTINUED		
Miscellaneous furniture and fixtures	259	9.39
Stone, clay, and glass products	32	11.68
Flat glass	321	16.51
Glass and glassware, pressed or blown	322	13.04
Glass containers	3221	13.76
Pressed and blown glass, nec	3229	12.36
Products of purchased glass	323	10.01
Cement, hydraulic	324	14.66
Structural clay products	325	9.98
Pottery and related products	326	10.16
Concrete, gypsum, and plaster products	327	11.30
Concrete block and brick	3271	10.68
Concrete products, nec	3272	10.15
Ready-mixed concrete	3273	12.00
Misc. nonmetallic mineral products	329	12.11
Abrasive products	3291	10.25
Asbestos products	3292	12.92
Fabricated metal products	34	11.41
Metal cans and shipping containers	341	15.00
Metalworking machinery	354	12.91
Machine tools, metal cutting types	3541	13.38
Machine tools, metal forming types	3542	12.91
Special dies, tools, jigs, and fixtures	3544	13.42
Machine tool accessories	3545	11.54
Electric lighting and wiring equipment	364	10.83
Electric lamps	3641	12.04
Current-carrying wiring devices	3643	10.76
Noncurrent-carrying wiring devices	3644	10.08
Residential lighting fixtures	3645	8.27
Household audio and video equipment	365	10.70
Household audio and video equipment	3651	11.00
Communications equipment	366	11.53
Telephone and telegraph apparatus	3661	12.18
Electronic components and accessories	367	11.00
Electron tubes	3671	12.54
Semiconductors and related devices	3674	13.95
Electronic components, nec	3679	9.73
Medical instruments and supplies	384	10.51
Surgical and medical instruments	3841	10.71
Surgical appliances and supplies	3842	9.96
Ophthalmic goods	385	8.50
Photographic equipment and supplies	386	14.79
Watches, clocks, watchcases, and parts	387	7.96
Miscellaneous manufacturing industries	39	9.08
Jewelry, silverware, and plated ware	391	9.54
Jewelry, precious metal	3911	9.52

NATIONAL AVERAGE HOURLY EARNINGS OF PRODUCTION OR NONSUPERVISORY WORKERS ON PRIVATE NONFARM PAYROLLS, BY SELECTED INDUSTRY (AUGUST 1992)—CONTINUED (NOT SEASONALLY ADJUSTED)

Industry	1987 SIC Code	Average hourly earnings
		August 1992
DURABLE GOODS—CONTINUED		
Musical instruments	393	8.89
Toys and sporting goods	394	8.39
Dolls, games, toys, and children's vehicles	3942,4	8.16
Sporting and athletic goods, nec	3949	8.55
Pens, pencils, office, and art supplies	395	9.93
Costume jewelry and notions	396	7.89
Costume jewelry	3961	6.96
Miscellaneous manufactures	399	9.54
Signs and advertising specialties	3993	9.91
NONDURABLE GOODS		10.70
Food and kindred products	20	10.13
Meat products	201	8.34
Meat packing plants	2011	9.19
Sausages and other prepared meats	2013	9.63
Poultry slaughtering and processing	2015	7.27
Dairy products	202	11.31
Cheese, natural and processed	2022	10.21
Fluid milk	2026	12.00
Preserved fruits and vegetables	203	9.56
Canned specialties	2032	12.56
Canned fruits and vegetables	2033	9.86
Frozen fruits and vegetables	2037	8.48
Grain mill products	204	12.09
Flour and other grain mill products	2041	10.98
Prepared feeds, nec	2048	9.80
Bakery products	205	11.51
Bread, cake, and related products	2051	11.46
Cookies, crackers, and frozen bakery products, except bread	2052,3	11.61
Sugar and confectionery products	206	11.26
Candy and other confectionery products	2064	9.49
Beverages	208	14.30
Malt beverages	2082	19.57
Bottled and canned soft drinks	2086	11.74
Misc. food and kindred products	209	9.29
Tobacco products	21	16.20
Cigarettes	211	20.96
Textile mill products	22	8.62
Broadwoven fabric mills, cotton	221	8.93
Broadwoven fabric mills, synthetics	222	9.29
Broadwoven fabric mills, wool	223	9.01
Narrow fabric mills	224	8.17
Knitting mills	225	7.92
Women's hosiery, except socks	2251	7.52
Hosiery, nec	2252	7.54

NATIONAL AVERAGE HOURLY EARNINGS OF PRODUCTION OR NONSUPERVISORY WORKERS ON PRIVATE NONFARM PAYROLLS, BY SELECTED INDUSTRY (AUGUST 1992)—CONTINUED (NOT SEASONALLY ADJUSTED)

Industry	1987 SIC Code	Average hourly earnings
		August 1992
NONDURABLE GOODS—CONTINUED		
Knit outerwear mills	2253	7.57
Knit underwear mills	2254	7.74
Weft knit fabric mills	2257	8.76
Textile finishing, except wool	226	9.02
Finishing plants, cotton	2261	8.99
Finishing plants, synthetics	2262	9.33
Carpets and rugs	227	8.58
Yarn and thread mills	228	8.34
Yarn spinning mills	2281	8.27
Throwing and winding mills	2282	8.72
Miscellaneous textile goods	229	10.11
Apparel and other textile products	23	6.96
Men's and boys' suits and coats	231	7.48
Men's and boys' furnishings	232	6.49
Men's and boys' shirts	2321	6.47
Men's and boys' trousers and slacks	2325	6.35
Men's and boys' work clothing	2326	6.31
Women's and misses' outerwear	233	6.56
Women's and misses' blouses and shirts	2331	6.00
Women's, juniors', and misses' dresses	2335	6.95
Women's and misses' suits and coats	2337	7.02
Women's and misses' outerwear, nec	2339	6.47
Women's and children's undergarments	234	6.75
Women's and children's underwear	2341	6.58
Brassieres, girdles, and allied garments	2342	7.66
Girls' and children's outerwear	236	6.33
Girls' and children's dresses and blouses	2361	6.31
Misc. apparel and accessories	238	6.79
Misc. fabricated textile products	239	8.35
Curtains and draperies	2391	7.05
House furnishings, nec	2392	7.11
Automotive and apparel trimmings	2396	11.04
Paper and allied products	23	6.96
Paper mills	262	16.06
Paperboard mills	263	16.16
Paperboard containers and boxes	265	10.99
Corrugated and solid fiber boxes	2653	11.12
Sanitary food containers	2656	10.98
Folding paperboard boxes	2657	11.62
Misc. converted paper products	267	11.48
Paper, coated and laminated, nec	2672	13.01
Bags: plastics, laminated, and coated	2673	10.88
Envelopes	2677	10.83
Printing and publishing	27	11.79
Newspapers	271	11.70
Periodicals	272	12.80

NATIONAL AVERAGE HOURLY EARNINGS OF PRODUCTION OR NONSUPERVISORY WORKERS ON PRIVATE NONFARM PAYROLLS, BY SELECTED INDUSTRY (AUGUST 1992)—CONTINUED (NOT SEASONALLY ADJUSTED)

Industry	1987 SIC Code	Average hourly earnings
		August 1992
NONDURABLE GOODS—CONTINUED		
Books	273	10.83
Book publishing	2731	10.49
Book printing	2732	11.21
Miscellaneous publishing	274	11.31
Commercial printing	275	11.99
Commercial printing, lithographic	2752	12.03
Commercial printing, nec	2759	11.78
Manifold business forms	276	12.56
Blankbooks and bookbinding	278	9.20
Printing trade services	279	14.18
Chemicals and allied products	28	14.47
Industrial inorganic chemicals	281	15.91
Industrial inorganic chemicals, nec	2819	16.14
Plastics materials and synthetics	282	15.40
Plastics materials and resins	2821	15.80
Organic fibers, noncellulosic	2824	14.80
Drugs	283	14.05
Pharmaceutical preparations	2834	14.06
Soap, cleaners, and toilet goods	284	11.97
Soap and other detergents	2841	15.57
Polishing, sanitation, and finishing preparations	2842,3	10.91
Toilet preparations	2844	10.31
Paints and allied products	285	12.53
Industrial organic chemicals	286	17.33
Cyclic crudes and intermediates	2865	17.05
Industrial organic chemicals, nec	2869	17.63
Agricultural chemicals	287	14.79
Miscellaneous chemical products	289	13.10
Rubber and misc. plastics products	30	10.38
Tires and inner tubes	301	16.78
Rubber and plastics footwear	309	7.53
Hose, belting, gaskets, and packing	305	10.29
Rubber and plastics hose and belting	3052	10.24
Fabricated rubber products, nec	306	9.76
Miscellaneous plastics products, nec	308	9.67
Leather and leather products	31	7.36
Leather tanning and finishing	311	9.55
Footwear, except rubber	314	6.98
Men's footwear, except athletic	3143	7.65
Women's footwear, except athletic	3144	6.46
Luggage	316	7.72
Handbags and personal leather goods	317	6.46
TRANSPORTATION AND PUBLIC UTILITIES		13.50
Trucking and warehousing	42	12.11
Trucking and courier services, except air	421	12.27

NATIONAL AVERAGE HOURLY EARNINGS OF PRODUCTION OR NONSUPERVISORY WORKERS ON PRIVATE NONFARM PAYROLLS, BY SELECTED INDUSTRY (AUGUST 1992)—CONTINUED (NOT SEASONALLY ADJUSTED)

Industry	1987 SIC Code	Average hourly earnings
		August 1992
TRANSPORTATION AND PUBLIC UTILITIES—CONTINUED		
Public warehousing and storage	422	9.93
Water transportation:		
Water transportation services	449	16.83
Pipelines, except natural gas	46	18.56
Transportation services	47	10.82
Passenger transportation arrangement	472	9.93
Travel agencies	4724	9.93
Freight transportation arrangement	473	12.08
Communications	48	14.51
Telephone communications	481	15.26
Radio and television broadcasting	483	13.79
Cable and other pay television services	484	10.99
Electric, gas, and sanitary services	49	16.05
Electric services	491	16.75
Gas production and distribution	492	15.40
Combination utility services	493	18.58
Sanitary services	495	11.97
WHOLESALE TRADE		11.43
Durable goods	50	11.78
Motor vehicles, parts, and supplies	501	10.44
Furniture and home furnishings	502	10.31
Lumber and other construction materials	503	11.05
Professional and commercial equipment	504	13.96
Medical and hospital equipment	5047	12.79
Metals and minerals, except petroleum	505	11.82
Electrical goods	506	12.21
Hardware, plumbing, and heating equipment	507	11.23
Machinery, equipment, and supplies	508	11.74
Misc. wholesale trade durable goods	509	9.15
Nondurable goods	51	10.96
Paper and paper products	511	11.54
WHOLESALE TRADE—CONTINUED		
Drugs, proprietaries, and sundries	512	13.15
Apparel, piece goods, and notions	513	10.59
Groceries and related products	514	11.10
Farm-product raw materials	515	8.16
Chemicals and allied products	516	13.21
Petroleum and petroleum products	517	10.52
Beer, wine, and distilled beverages	518	12.85
Misc. wholesale trade nondurable goods	519	9.33
RETAIL TRADE		7.10
Building materials and garden supplies	52	8.44
Lumber and other building materials	521	8.80

NATIONAL AVERAGE HOURLY EARNINGS OF PRODUCTION OR NONSUPERVISORY WORKERS ON PRIVATE NONFARM PAYROLLS, BY SELECTED INDUSTRY (AUGUST 1992)—CONTINUED (NOT SEASONALLY ADJUSTED)

Industry	1987 SIC Code	Average hourly earnings
		August 1992
RETAIL TRADE—CONTINUED		
Hardware stores	525	7.20
Retail nurseries and garden stores	526	7.40
General merchandise stores	53	7.18
Department stores	531	7.23
Variety stores	533	6.02
Misc. general merchandise stores	539	7.58
Food stores	54	7.51
Grocery stores	541	7.59
Retail bakeries	546	6.70
Automotive dealers and service stations	55	9.40
New and used car dealers	551	11.78
Auto and home supply stores	553	8.16
Gasoline service stations	554	6.50
Automotive dealers, nec	559	11.00
Apparel and accessory stores	56	6.84
Men's and boys' clothing stores	561	8.40
Women's clothing stores	562	6.43
Family clothing stores	565	6.65
Shoe stores	566	7.10
Furniture and home furnishings stores	57	9.25
Furniture and home furnishings stores	571	9.06
Household appliance stores	572	9.71
Radio, television, and computer stores	573	9.44
Radio, television, and electronic stores	5731	9.18
Record and prerecorded tape stores	5735	5.91
Eating and drinking places	58	5.28
Miscellaneous retail establishments	59	7.63
Drug stores and proprietary stores	591	7.61
Used merchandise stores	593	6.53
Miscellaneous shopping goods stores	594	7.08
Nonstore retailers	596	8.24
Fuel dealers	598	10.63
Retail stores, nec	599	8.01
FINANCE, INSURANCE, AND REAL ESTATE		10.84
Depository institutions	60	8.97
Commercial banks	602	8.60
Credit unions	606	8.78
Nondepository institutions	61	11.62
Personal credit institutions	614	9.99
Security and commodity brokers:		
Security and commodity services	628	15.17
Insurance carriers	63	12.47
Life insurance	631	11.37
Medical service and health insurance	632	11.98
Fire, marine, and casualty insurance	633	13.46

NATIONAL AVERAGE HOURLY EARNINGS OF PRODUCTION OR NONSUPERVISORY WORKERS ON PRIVATE NONFARM PAYROLLS, BY SELECTED INDUSTRY (AUGUST 1992)—CONTINUED (NOT SEASONALLY ADJUSTED)

Industry	1987 SIC Code	Average hourly earnings
		August 1992
SERVICES		10.45
Agricultural services	07	8.16
Hotels and other lodging places:		
Hotels and motels	701	7.24
Personal services:		
Laundry, cleaning, and garment services	721	7.18
Beauty shops	723	7.68
Miscellaneous personal services	729	7.85
Business services	73	9.96
Advertising	731	15.10
Mailing, reproduction, and stenographic services:		
Photocopying and duplicating services	7334	9.36
Services to buildings	734	7.39
Miscellaneous equipment		
rental and leasing	735	10.41
Heavy construction equipment rental	7353	13.52
Personnel supply services:		
Help supply services	7363	8.26
Computer and data processing services	737	15.89
Computer programming services	7371	18.27
Computer integrated systems design	7373	16.67
Information retrieval services	7375	13.06
Computer maintenance and repair	7378	13.65
Miscellaneous business services	738	8.54
Detective and armored car services	7381	6.71
Security systems services	7382	10.22
Auto repair, services, and parking	75	9.16
Automobile parking	752	8.85
Automotive repair shops	753	10.07
Miscellaneous repair services	76	10.83
Motion pictures	78	11.69
Motion picture production and services	781	17.96
Amusement and recreation services	79	7.45
Bowling centers	793	6.61
Misc. amusement and recreation services	799	6.97
Physical fitness facilities	7991	7.83
Membership sports and recreation clubs	7997	7.41
Health services	80	11.40
Offices and clinics of medical doctors	801	11.42
Offices and clinics of dentists	802	10.97
Offices and clinics of other health		
practitioners	804	9.95
Nursing and personal care facilities	805	7.85
Intermediate care facilities	8052	7.24
Hospitals	806	13.08
Home health care services	808	9.98
Legal services	81	15.15

NATIONAL AVERAGE HOURLY EARNINGS OF PRODUCTION OR NONSUPERVISORY WORKERS ON PRIVATE NONFARM PAYROLLS, BY SELECTED INDUSTRY (AUGUST 1992)—CONTINUED (NOT SEASONALLY ADJUSTED)

Industry	1987 SIC Code	Average hourly earnings
		August 1992
SERVICES—CONTINUED		
Social services:		
Child day care services	835	6.38
Membership organizations:		
Professional organizations	862	14.43
Engineering and management services	87	14.79
Engineering and architectural services	871	16.05
Engineering services	8711	16.64
Architectural services	8712	14.89
Surveying services	8713	11.07
Accounting, auditing, and bookkeeping	872	13.35
Research and testing services	873	15.55
Management and public relations	874	13.40
Public relations services	8743	13.85
Services, nec	89	15.95

CHAPTER 16

STATE HEALTH CARE REFORMS

While the debate over federal health care reforms continues in fits and starts, a host of state legislatures have quietly set about reforming health insurance on a local level. While many states have established commissions that have proposed far-reaching reforms, the actual legislation to date has been more practical and is mostly limited to the following two issues:

Rate Reform: As explained in Chapter Two, some insurance industry practices that can make insurance inaccessible to small businesses are excluding unhealthy individuals or charging very high premiums to groups with such individuals. Rate reform rules restrict how much insurers can vary rates between sick and healthy employees, limit rate increases due to past claims experience or health status, and prohibit insurers from rejecting employees or groups. Many states also prohibit insurers from canceling individuals or groups because they have high medical expenses.

Exemptions from state mandates for small groups: One of the reasons health care costs so much is that some states require insurance companies to include certain "mandated" benefits in their policies. As a result, any employer who purchases insurance has no choice but to pay for these benefits. Mandated benefits commonly include coverage for newborns, treatment for drug or alcohol abuse, mammograms, and treatment by chiropractors and podiatrists. Other mandated benefits range from the bizarre to the absurd: acupuncture, hair transplants, sex-change operations, and treatment by herbal medicine. Mandates can boost rates by 17 to 20 percent.

But many states are now relaxing the rules on mandated benefits for small businesses and are allowing insurers to offer less expensive "no-frills" policies.

STATE HEALTH CARE REFORMS

Following is a summary of the small group reforms that each state has adopted. The term "health status" is used to signify either the past claims experience of the group or the current medical conditions of the group's members. Most of the rating reforms are being phased in over the next few years. There are a lot of changes going on, so check with your local state insurance department for the latest rules.

Arizona

HB 2027 allows no-frills policies for groups with 25 or fewer employees.

Arkansas

No-frills policies are allowed for all group sizes. Initial rates and renewal rate increases based on health status are limited for groups of 1 to 25 employees; insurers are not allowed to cancel policies because of health status.

California

Initial rates and renewal rate increases based on health status are limited for groups of 3 to 50; insurers are not allowed to cancel policies because of health status.

Colorado

No-frills policies are allowed for groups of 1 to 25 employees. Rates can vary with current health status for groups of 1 to 25, but only for conditions existing for less than 5 years; insurers are not allowed to cancel policies because of health status.

Connecticut

Rating according to claims experience is limited for groups of 1 to 25; insurers are not allowed to cancel policies or reject applicants because of health status.

Delaware

Initial rates and renewal rate increases based on health status are limited for groups of 1 to 25; insurers are not allowed to cancel policies or reject applicants for groups of 2 to 25 because of health status.

Florida

No-frills policies are allowed for groups with under 25 employees. Initial rates and renewal rate increases based on health status are limited for groups of 1 to 25; insurers are not allowed to cancel policies because of health status; insurers are not allowed to reject applicants because of health status. Florida is moving in the direction of "play-or-pay": employers either buy coverage or pay a wage tax to buy into a government insurance program.

Georgia

No-frills policies are allowed. Rating according to claims experience is limited for groups of 1 to 50; insurers are not allowed to cancel policies because of health status.

Hawaii

For many years, Hawaii has required most employers to provide coverage to employees. Employees contribute to costs. Dependent coverage is optional.

Illinois

No-frills policies are allowed for groups with fewer than 26 employees.

Indiana

Initial rates and rate increases based on health status are limited for groups of 3 to 25; insurers are not allowed to cancel policies because of health status.

Iowa

No-frills policies are allowed for groups of under 26. Initial rates and renewal rate increases based on health status are limited for groups of 1 to 25 with at least 2 covered employees at time of issue, but the regulators have authority to relax the rules; insurers are not allowed to cancel policies or reject applicants because of health status.

Kansas

No-frills policies are allowed for groups of under 26. Rates and rate increases based on health status are limited for groups of 1 to 25; insurers are not allowed to cancel policies or reject applicants for groups of 3 to 25 because of health status.

Kentucky

No-frills policies are allowed for groups of under 51.

Louisiana

Initial rates and renewal rate increases for health status are limited for groups of 1 to 35; insurers are not allowed to cancel policies because of health status.

Maine

By mid-1997, insurers will not be allowed to consider age, sex, industry, or geographic locale when setting rates for groups of 1 to 24. These rules must be confirmed by mid-1994 or they will be automatically repealed. Insurers are not allowed to cancel policies or reject applicants because of health status.

Maryland

No-frills policies are allowed for groups of 2 to 25.

Massachusetts

Initial rates and renewal rate increases based on health status are limited for groups of 1 to 25; insurers are not allowed to cancel policies or reject applicants because of health status. Earlier "play-or-pay" legislation that required employers to either buy coverage or pay a wage tax to buy into a government insurance program has run into budgetary roadblocks.

Massachusetts seems to be moving in the direction of community rating; that is, insurance rates will not vary by age, sex, or health status.

Minnesota

Comprehensive health care reform has passed in Minnesota that aims to reduce the number of uninsured. Initial rates based on health status, sex, or industry are limited for groups of 2 to 29; insurers are not allowed to cancel policies or decline applicants because of health status.

Missouri

No-frills policies are allowed for groups of under 51 employees. For groups of 3 to 25, initial rates and renewal rate increases based on health status are limited; insurers are not allowed to cancel policies or decline applicants because of health status.

Montana

No-frills policies are allowed for groups with fewer than 21 employees.

Nebraska

No-frills policies are allowed for groups of under 26 employees. Initial rates and renewal rate increases based on health status are limited for groups of 1 to 25; insurers are not allowed to cancel policies because of health status.

Nevada

No-frills policies are allowed for groups of under 26 employees.

New Hampshire

Initial rates and renewal rate increases based on health status are limited for groups of 2 to 50 employees.

New Jersey

No-frills policies are allowed for any size group. New Jersey has adopted legislation that will require community rating of groups of 2 to 49 by 1997; rates will then be set without considering the age, sex, residence, occupation, or health status of the employees.

New Mexico

No-frills policies are allowed for groups of under 20 employees. Initial rates and renewal rate increases based on health status are limited for groups of 1 to 25 employees.

New York

Insurers may not vary rates by age, sex, industry, or health status for groups with 1 to 50 employees. Insurers must sell policies to any applicant.

Preexisting conditions may not be excluded if the individual previously had coverage (subject to conditions).

North Carolina

No-frills policies are allowed for groups with fewer than 26 employees. Initial rates and renewal rate increases based on health status are limited for groups of 3 to 25; insurers are not allowed to cancel policies or reject applicants because of health status.

North Dakota

No-frills policies are allowed for groups of under 25 employees. Initial rates and renewal rate increases based on health status are limited for groups of 1 to 25; insurers are not allowed to cancel policies because of health status.

Oregon

No-frills policies are allowed for groups with fewer than 26 employees. Initial rates and renewal rate increases based on health status are limited for groups with 3 to 25 employees; insurers are not allowed to cancel policies or reject applicants because of health status.

Pennsylvania

Exclusion of individuals from groups is forbidden, either at the time of group inception or for new entrants.

Rhode Island

No-frills policies are allowed for groups with fewer than 26 employees. Initial rates and renewal rate increases due to health status are limited for groups of 1 to 50. Insurers are not allowed to cancel policies or reject applicants for groups of 3 to 25 because of health status.

South Carolina

Initial rates and renewal rate increases based on health status are limited for groups of 1 to 25; insurers are not allowed to cancel policies because of health status.

South Dakota

Initial rates and renewal rate increases based on health status are limited for groups of 1 to 25; insurers are not allowed to cancel policies because of health status.

Tennessee

Initial rates and renewal rate increases based on health status are limited for groups of 3 to 25; insurers are not allowed to cancel policies or reject applicants because of health status.

Vermont

Insurers may not vary rates for age, sex, locale, industry, or health status without the prior permission of state regulators for groups with 1 to 19 employees. They are not allowed to cancel policies or reject applicants because of health status.

Virginia

No-frills policies are allowed for groups of under 50 employees. Insurers are prohibited from excluding individuals because of health status for groups of 2 to 50 employees; they are not allowed to cancel policies because of health status.

Washington

No-frills policies are allowed for groups with fewer than 25 employees.

West Virginia

No-frills policies are allowed for all size groups. Initial rates and renewal rate increases based on health status are limited for groups of 2 to 59; insurers are not allowed to cancel policies because of health status.

Wisconsin

Initial rates and renewal rate increases based on health status are limited for groups of 2 to 25; insurers are not allowed to cancel policies or reject applicants because of health status.

Wyoming

Initial rates and renewal rate increases based on health status are limited for groups of 2 to 25; insurers are not allowed to cancel policies or reject applicants because of health status.

GLOSSARY

While we've tried to keep insurance-ese to a minimum in this book, we can't control what gets produced by insurance companies. Here is a glossary to figure out some of the various expressions used by the industry.

Accidental death and dismemberment insurance: (AD&D) A kind of insurance plan that pays the face amount upon death due to accidental causes (as opposed to sickness) or will pay some fraction of the face amount for the accidental loss of use of a hand, foot, or eyesight.

Adverse selection: Tendency for individuals to purchase benefits they are likely to use, resulting in increased costs to the insurer.

Blue Cross and Blue Shield plans: Generally non-profit health plans, part of the Blue Cross/Blue Shield Association, which typically enroll all applicants regardless of health. Each operates independently in a specific geographic area. Participating physicians and hospitals agree to accept predetermined fees.

Cafeteria plans: A type of flexible benefit plan that permits an employee to determine how an employer's and his own contributions will be allocated among the benefits offered.

Career average formula: One alternative way to set up a defined benefit pension plan (see below). Participants' benefits may be a percentage of pay for each year they participate or based on a percentage of career average pay multiplied by their years of service.

Child care: (See dependent care)

Cliff vesting: One approach to calculating the point at which the employee is entitled to employer contributions to a pension plan. (Employee contributions under any plan are immediately vested.) Under minimum Federal cliff vesting standards, there is no vesting for five years, then 100% vesting.

COBRA (Consolidated Omnibus Budget Reconciliation Act of 1985): Among other things requires employers with health plans to offer employees continued access to group health benefits when they lose coverage due to terminating employment (except in cases of gross misconduct.) Special rules apply to dental and vision coverage. The former employee would have to pay for coverage.

Coinsurance: A requirement that the covered employee or dependent pays a certain percentage—commonly 20%—of eligible medical expenses with the plan covering the rest.

Comprehensive Major Medical: A design for medical benefits that typically covers many aspects of medical care, but requires the covered person to pay a deductible and coinsurance.

Community rating: An insurance rate based on the experience of a large community of covered persons, not just the members of the group being insured.

Conversion privilege: A provision of the insurance contract which permits an insured person to continue coverage on a direct payment basis after leaving a group.

Coordination of benefits: Reduces the benefit under one insurance contract if similar benefits are available under the second contract. Typically used when both spouses in a couple have health coverage. The procedure allows carriers to limit payments to no more than 100% of the actual charges.

Death benefits (See *Survivor benefits*)

Deductibles: A specified amount of initial medical costs that an individual must pay before any expenses are reimbursed by the health plan.

Defined benefit plans: Each employee's retirement benefit is determined by a specific formula and the plan provides a guaranteed level of benefits on retirement.

Defined contribution plans: The retirement benefit is the total of employer and employee contributions, investment gains or losses, and gains or losses from the operation of the pension fund.

Dental care plans: Covers certain procedures of dental care for employees and sometimes dependents, including diagnostic, preventive, restorative, and corrective care.

Dependents: Spouses and children of an employee covered by insurance; usually dependent children are covered to age 19, older if full-time students.

Diagnosis related group: One of about 500 groupings of diagnoses of ailments established for Medicare patients and others as a way of keeping costs down. If the cost of care exceeds the Medicare limit for the DRG, the hospital "eats" the rest of the cost.

Disability income plans: Insurance which replaces a portion of the worker's income lost as a result of a disability. Work-related disabilities are also covered by workers' compensation insurance.

Education assistance benefits: Employer reimbursement for some or all of the cost of college courses, usually those related to a job.

Employee assistance programs: Counseling services directed at acute personal problems that hinder job performance, such as drug and alcohol abuse and financial and emotional problems.

ERISA (Employment Retirement Income Security Act of 1974): Establishes standards that employee benefit plans must follow to get and maintain their tax favored status. Establishes contribution and benefit limits for retirement plans.

Employee stock ownership plans: Permits companies to share ownership with employees through the contribution of company stock without requiring the employees to invest their own money. Can also be used to borrow money to finance corporations, a perk that came under Congressional attack in 1989 when the large amount of debt incurred by some ESOPs was connected with heavy takeover activity.

Evidence of insurability: Data on medical history submitted by an individual seeking coverage under medical, life or disability plans. Adverse information could result in either being excluded from coverage, included only after a waiting period, paying more for coverage, or receiving limited coverage.

Experience rating: The setting of a group's insurance premiums, partially or wholly on the basis of the claims experience of the members of the group.

Explanation of benefits: A form provided to patients by their insurer after a claim has been paid, enabling the patient to check not only benefits received but also the services for which the provider has requested compensation.

Fee for service: A billing system in which a physician or hospital charges for each service rendered. This system contrasts with the prepayment approach (HMOs, PPOs), wherein medical care providers are paid flat fees based on expected costs.

401(k) plans: A retirement savings plan which permits the employee to contribute pretax income, with income tax deferred until the money is taken out. Employers may also make contributions.

Flexible benefit plans: (See *Cafeteria plans*)

Gatekeeper physicians: Those primary care doctors in many HMOs and PPOs who control referrals to specialists and hospitals as a method of cost containment.

Group life insurance plan: A life insurance benefit provided to employees by employers, usually making lump-sum distributions to a designated beneficiary or beneficiaries.

Group model HMOs: A group practice of physicians who contract to service HMO patients; part of the time is spent in private practice. Distinct from staff model HMOs, in which the doctors are employed by the HMO, so all of their time is spent treating HMO patients.

Guaranteed investment contracts (GICs): Investments similar to Certificates of Deposit (CDs) purchased from insurance companies. One of the primary investments of 401(k) plans.

Health maintenance organization (HMO): A provider and financer of medical care contracts with a limited number of doctors and hospitals and which emphasizes preventative care and early intervention. Advocates say it is a better approach to cost containment than the conventional fee-for-service approach, because doctors have an incentive to practice efficiently.

Income averaging: A method of figuring out how much tax you owe on a lump sum distribution of a qualified pension plan.

Independent practice associations: A kind of HMO that contracts with individual physicians to provide services to HMO members. These physicians provide some services to HMO members but also treat other patients. Distinct from the group model HMOs (see above) and staff model HMOs (see below).

Individual retirement accounts (IRAs): An individual retirement plan that enables workers to save money on a tax deferred basis. Although all people working for employers who don't offer a pension plan can deduct their contributions up to $2,000, the Tax Reform Act of 1986 limited full deductibility of those who are already covered by a pension plan to individuals whose adjusted gross income doesn't exceed $25,000 and married taxpayers filing jointly to $40,000. (Contributions are partially deductible for singles up to $35,000 and couples up to $50,000.)

Keogh plans: Permits unincorporated small business owners to participate in tax-qualified plans similar to those of corporate employers. The self-employed may either be sole proprietors or members of a partnership.

Key employees: A criterion used to describe highly compensated officers or owners of companies and used to establish whether a defined benefit pension plan is top heavy; if it is, special requirements for vesting, contributions and benefits must be met to retain tax qualifications.

Major medical: Supplemental coverage to basic hospital and surgical-medical coverage designed to take care of a broad scope of extra medical and hospital costs. Major medical plans usually have a deductible and coinsurance payable by the subscriber. These costs include physician home visits, drugs, etc.

Money purchase plans: A defined contribution pension plan in which employer contributions are mandatory and are usually stated as a percentage of salary.

Multi-employer trust or multi-employer welfare association: A grouping of companies created for the purpose of financing insurance-type benefits. Controversial because they fall into a regulatory gray area and many have foundered. Refer to Chapter Three.

Non-discrimination rules: Tax-qualified pension plans must make sure that the plans aren't overly generous to highly compensated employees.

Open enrollment: A limited period of time during which new subscribers can enroll for benefits or current subscribers can change benefits without undergoing special underwriting or limitations on coverage.

Out-of-pocket expenses: That part of medical bills paid by the patient/employee.

Preexisting conditions: Health conditions that were known to exist at the time the employee joined the plan. Some plans may cover these conditions after a waiting period of six months or so; some plans may never cover the condition.

Preferred provider organizations: Contractual arrangements between health care providers and either an employer or an insurance company to provide fee-for-service health care, usually at a discount.

Profit sharing plan: A defined contribution pension plan in which contributions are typically derived from a portion of company profits, although contributions can be made in unprofitable years and skipped in prosperous years.

Screening: Testing for the presence of specific health problems, such as high blood pressure, in a well population. Used as part of a corporate wellness program.

Self-insurance: The practice of choosing not to purchase health insurance but instead to pay claims as they occur and purchase stop-loss coverage to protect against catastrophic expenses. Technically not insurance, except for the stop-loss coverage.

Sick leave: A policy that continues to pay wages while an employee is sick for a short time, usually a specified number of days each year. Sick leave covers some of the waiting period before the employee is eligible for short-term disability coverage.

Simplified employee pension: A company sponsored Individual Retirement Account (IRA) that permits a larger employee contribution. Can be employer- or employee-funded.

Stock bonus plan: A defined contribution pension plan in which contributions and benefit payments are made in the form of company stock.

Stop-loss coverage: Insurance that pays for claims larger than a specified amount. Often used to limit the risk of self-insured benefit programs.

Subscriber: An insured person.

Target benefit plan: Similar to a defined benefit plan except that contributions are made to an individual account. Employer promises to make the required contributions to add up to the right amount at retirement time, but doesn't guarantee that the amount will be there.

Third party payer: Any organization that pays or insures medical expenses.

Third party administrator: A company other than an insurer that processes claims and/or performs other administrative activities associated with the benefit plan.

Thrift or savings plan: A defined contribution pension plan which is essentially an employee savings account, often with employer matching contributions.

Underwriting: Process of evaluating risk. This may mean evaluating employees and their dependents to determine premium rates and possible coverage limits.

Waiting period: A period of time an individual must wait before becoming eligible for a given benefit after employment has begun.

Workers' compensation: Benefits for workers who are disabled by occupational illness or injury. Effectively required by law in every state.

CREDITS

INTRODUCTION

Health care spending statistics are from EBRI Databook on Employee Benefits, second edition, 1992.

Quotes from Arnold Relman are from "A Doctor's Advice on Cost Containment," *Across the Board,* October 1989.

Mental health data are from "Managed Mental Health Care Issues and Strategies," by Robin Weiner and Debra Siegel, *Benefits Quarterly,* Third Quarter, 1989.

Statistics from the Blues on increased doctor visits are from "Managing the High Cost of Health Care," *Black Enterprise,* October 1988.

Statistics on the working uninsured are from *Why Are Group Health Benefits Such a Big Problem for Small Business?,* Council of Smaller Enterprises, 1989.

Heritage Foundation health care proposal is from "Nationalized Health Care Isn't a Cure," *The (Bergen County, New Jersey) Record,* February 26, 1989.

Alain Enthoven's proposal is from "In Search of Health Care Access and Affordability," *Best's Review,* June 1990.

Additional Relman quote is from "Reforming the Health Care System," *The New England Journal of Medicine,* October 4, 1990.

Statistics on Canadian health care and quote from *Maclean's* magazine are from "Health Care, Canadian-Style," *Nation's Business,* September 1989.

Information about Heartbeat Windsor and William Byng quote are from "Canadians Cross the Border to Save Their Lives," *Nation's Business,* September 1990.

HIAA survey is from "Canada's Health Plan Is Not for Importing," *Wall Street Journal, December 1990.*

Blendon quote is from "Employers Must be Pro-Active in Choosing Health Care," *Gannett Westchester Newspapers,* March 20, 1989.

CHAPTER TWO

Statistics on Blues' loss of market share and collapse of West Virginia plan from "First Blue Cross Collapse in U.S. Puts Policyholders in Dire Straits," *Wall Street Journal Europe*, March 12, 1991.

Statistics on HMOs and PPOs are from *Fundamentals of Employee Benefits*, Fourth Edition, by the Employee Benefit Research Institute, an EBRI-ERF Publication, 1990.

Foster Higgins survey results on HMOs are from "Curbing the High Cost of Health Care," *Nation's Business*, September 1989.

Mahoney quote is from "Curbing the High Cost of Health Care," *Nation's Business*, September 1989.

CHAPTER THREE

ERISA data on METs from "Federal Control of MEWAS Advised," *Business Insurance*, October 29, 1990.

First Sam Nunn quote is from "MEWAs Targeted at Senate Hearing," *Employee Benefit Plan Review*, July 1990.

Second Sam Nunn quote is from "Beware of Scams," *Medical Benefits*, July 15, 1990.

Quote from Jo Hardwick is from "Senate Looking into Some Health-Insurance Pooling," *Wall Street Journal*, May 15, 1990.

Anecdote about Texas MEWA is from "Beware of Scams," *Nation's Business*, July 1990.

Anecdote about North Carolina MEWA is from "Hazardous to Your Health," *Financial World*, August 21, 1990.

Anecdote about Georgia MEWA and quote from Scott Kyle is from "MEWA Mischief," *Barron's*, March 19, 1990.

James Long quote is from "MEWAs Targeted at Senate Hearing," *Employee Benefit Plan Review*, July 1990.

Robert Turell quote is from "Seeking Affordable Health Care Taxes Many a Firm's Ingenuity," *Los Angeles Times*, February 16, 1990.

Anecdote about Panel Processing is from "Mounting Health Costs Spur Creativity," *Business Insurance*, March 19, 1990.

Sandmeyer Steel anecdote is from "Help Wanted," *Inc.*, December 1989.

Joyce Wans quote is from "Expert Views Pros, Cons of Self-Insurance," *Business Insurance*, October 29, 1990.

Anecdote about Council of Small Enterprises is from "Seeking Affordable Health Care Taxes Many a Firm's Ingenuity," *Los Angeles Times*, February 16, 1990.

CHAPTER FOUR

Rand Corporation study is from "Curbing the High Cost of Health Care," *Nation's Business*, September 1989.

GAO data and statistics on firms dropping retiree health benefits are from "Sick and Tired of the Retiree Tab," *The* (Bergen County, New Jersey) *Record*, July 9, 1990.

Michigan Spring anecdote is from "A Flexible Benefit Program That Works," *Small Business Reports*, November 1988.

CHAPTER SIX

American Journal of Public Health data are from "Wellness Programs Are Promoted by More Firms," *Wall Street Journal*, January 17, 1989.

Traveler's Insurance and University of Michigan smoking data are from "Assessing the Corporate Fitness Craze," *New York Times*, March 18, 1990.

Statistics about success of wellness programs are from "Employers Celebrate Employee Fitness," *Business Insurance*, May 21, 1990.

Control Data Study from "Help Wanted," *Inc.*, December 1989.

Data on relationship between smokers and health claims are from "Wellness Works for Small Firms," *Nation's Business*, December 1989.

Insurance discounts from Travelers and John Alden are from "Help Wanted," *Inc.*, December 1989.

Anecdote about Scherer Brothers is from "Wellness Works for Small Firms," *Nation's Business*, December 1989.

Southern California Edison anecdote is from "Companies Tie Benefits to Wellness," *Washington Post*, March 11, 1990.

Statistics on utility's costs dropping are from "Firms urge the wellness habit," *Boston Globe*, July 16, 1990.

Data on Provident Indemnity Life, Safeway Bakery, First Interstate Bank, Plaskolite, Stevens Real Estate, Bodolay Pratt are from *Wellness in Small Business*, Washington Business Group on Health, 1985.

Data on Quaker Oats' wellness program is from "Wellness Plans: An Ounce of Prevention," *Newsweek*, January 30, 1989.

Anecdotes about Fitness Plus Inc. are from "Assessing the Corporate Fitness Craze," *New York Times*, March 18, 1990.

Anecdotes about Baker Hughes Inc., U-Haul, Pointe Resorts and Southern California Edison are from "Better Benefits for the Fittest," *Washington Post*, March 11, 1990.

Data on Pennzoil's screening program are from "Cancer Screening Pays Off," *Industry Week*, February 15, 1988.

Carol Biederman anecdote is from "Firms Urge the Wellness Habit," *Boston Globe*, Monday July 16, 1990.

Data about Maupintour is from "Help Wanted," *Inc*, December 1989.

Data on Johnson & Johnson's health program is from "Wellness Now a Watchword for Workers," *Atlanta Constitution*, March 20, 1989.

CHAPTER SEVEN

Description of nonoccupational temporary disability benefits, application of ADEA to disability benefits is from *Fundamentals of Employee Benefits*, Fourth Edition, EBRI-ERF Publications, 1990.

Information about integrating coverage with other benefits is from *Employee Benefit Planning* by Terry Rosenbloom and Victor Hallman, Prentice Hall, New York (1986).

CHAPTER EIGHT

Jose C. anecdote is from "Small Firms Find Workers' Compensation to be Painful," *Wall Street Journal*, June 22, 1989.

John Burton quote is from "Fighting the High Cost of Workers' Comp," *Nation's Business*, March 1990.

Expenditures on workers' compensation insurance are from "Fewer Blank Checks to Cover Job Injuries," *Wall Street Journal*, August 10, 1990.

Data on assigned risk pools are from *Responding to the Workers' Compensation Crisis*, a survey by Tillinghast, a unit of Towers, Perrin.

Employer's financial obligations are from "Should Small Business Self-Insure Workers' Compensation?," *Small Business Reports*, November 1988.

Department of Labor data from "State Workers' Compensation: Legislation Enacted in 1990," *Monthly Labor Review*, January 1991.

Roger Stephens quote, BLS statistics are from *Business Insurance*, September 10, 1990.

David Cochran quote, Theodore Braun quote, David Eisen quote are from, "Employers Can Reduce Risk of Injury," *Business Insurance*, September 19, 1990.

Linda Morse quote is from "What Sufferers Can Do About That Pain in the Wrist," *Business Week*, January 29, 1990.

CHAPTER NINE

John Satagaj, Barbara Judy, Barbara Balter quotes are from "Removing Barriers for the Handicapped," *Washington Post*, August 13, 1990.

Mariott Corp., Sears Roebuck anecdotes, Motley quote, data from National Association of Convenience Stores are from "Disabled-Rights Bill Inspires Hope, Fear," *Wall Street Journal*, May 23, 1990.

Bank of Montreal, Honeywell anecdotes are from "Mastering the Language of Disability," *New York Times*, February 10, 1991.

Patrisha Wright quote from "Doors Opening for the Disabled," *Washington Post*, May 25, 1990.

CHAPTER TEN

Anecdotes about pizza maker and nonprofit organization are from "AIDS/ Why You Can't Afford to Ignore It," *Automotive Executive*, February 1990.

Data on lawsuits filed by people with AIDS are from "Small Business Cannot Afford to Remain Silent on a Policy for AIDs," *Business and Health*, February 1989.

Alexander & Alexander Consulting Group survey and Becky Padget quote are from "Businesses Facing Up to Realities of AIDS," *Atlanta Constitution*, October 6, 1988.

Paul Kaplan quote is from "AIDS in the Workplace," *Nation's Business*, August 1987.

Laws companies must observe in dealing with workers with AIDS are from "What Do You Know About AIDS in the Workplace?," *American Ink Maker*, April 1990.

Anita Schoomaker quote is from "AIDS/Why You Can't Afford to Ignore It," *Automotive Executive*, February 1990.

Ira Singer quote is from "Operators Must Face Fear of AIDS," *Convenience Store News*, May 6-May 30, 1988.

Citizens Commission on AIDS for New York City and Northern New Jersey is from "AIDS Concerns for Business," *Nation's Business*, June 1989.

Ben Strohecker anecdote is from "AIDS/ Why You Can't Afford to Ignore It," *Automotive Executive*, February 1990.

David Herold quote is from "With AIDS, Little Knowledge is Worse Than None," *Wall Street Journal*, February 14, 1989.

Anecdote about Pacific Bell is from "Dealing With AIDS in the Workplace," *Los Angeles Times*, May 7, 1989.

General Motors anecdote and information on Digital Equipment Corp. and Levis Strauss is from "A Businesslike Approach to AIDS," *U.S. News & World Report*, April 2, 1990.

Larry anecdote is from "AIDS: Where Insurers Are Showing Little Mercy," *Business Week*, November 21, 1988.

Data from the National Center for Health Services and Health Technology Assessment is from "AIDS Concerns for Business," *Nation's Business*, June 1989.

Johnson & Higgins survey is from "AIDS in the Workplace," *Nation's Business*, August 1987.

Warren Greenberg quote is from "AIDS Concerns for Business," *Nation's Business*, June 1989.

Data on life insurance costs and recommendations for handling certain categories of workers is from *AIDS/Its Impact on Your Business*, by the Philadelphia Commission on AIDS and the Greater Philadelphia Chamber of Commerce, June 1988.

CHAPTER ELEVEN

Sawyer Gas anecdote is from "Small Firms Enlist to Fight Drugs," *Nation's Business*, February 1990.

Data about the Drug Free Workplace Act is from "Drug-Free Law Catches Employers Off Guard," *Boston Globe*, May 15, 1989.

Material on The President's Commission on Organized Crime, Charles Schumer quote are from "Battling the Enemy Within," *Time*, March 17, 1986.

Data on workers' compensation legislation is from "Six States Take Action on Workplace Drug Laws," *Drug Free Workplace Report*, Fall 1990.

Marijuana survey by Kaim Associates is from "Marijuana Bigger Threat Than Cocaine: Study," *Business Insurance*, September 3, 1990.

Daniel Burke quote is from "Battling the Enemy Within," *Time*, March 17, 1986.

Workplace Consultants' survey and Carroll quote is from "Drug Proofing the Workplace: A Guide for Supervisors," is from *Supervisory Management*, October 1989.

De Bernardo quotes that begin "those who are unable . . ." and "local police should . . ." are from "On the Job Against Drugs," *Nation's Business*, July 1989.

Tom Warner quote is from "Solving Substance Abuse in the Workplace," *Washington Post*, May 28, 1990.

Peter Bensinger quote, EAP data are from "Battling the Enemy Within," *Time*, March 17, 1986.

Data on small business efforts in Washington, Maryland and Missouri is from "Small Firms Enlist to Fight Drugs," *Nation's Business*, February 1990.

Daniel Burke quote is from "Battling the Enemy Within," *Time*, March 17, 1986.

Drug testing statistics are from "On the Job Against Drugs," *Nation's Business*, July 1989.

Midwest utility and DIY chain's drug-testing policy are from *Business Insurance*, September 3, 1990.

CHAPTER THIRTEEN

Data on the percentage of companies that offer pension plans is from *Fundamentals of Employee Benefit Programs*, Employee Benefit Research Institute, 1990.

Data on "dropouts" from pension plans is from a study for the SBA entitled *Cost and Impact of Federal Regulation on Small Versus Large Business Retirement Plans*, by James Bell Associates Inc. and Lewin/ICF, June 1990.

Data on NFIB study is from *Pension Policy and Small Employers: At What Price Coverage?*, by Employee Benefit Research Institute, 1989.

Sheeran anecdote is from "We're in the Money," *Inc.*, November 1984.

Two ways of determining employer contributions to profit sharing plans and vesting formulas are from *Employee Benefit and Retirement Planning*, Stephan Leimberg and John McFadden, The National Underwriter Co., 1989.

DOL statistics on popularity of deferred profit-sharing plans and statistics on 401(k)s are from *Fundamentals of Employee Benefit Programs*, Employee Benefit Research Institute, 1990.

Tips on how to set up a SEP are from the pamphlet *Simplified Employee Pensions/What Small Businesses Need to Know*, by the U.S. Department of Labor and the Small Business Administration.

Mark Rayford quote, estimates on plan administrator fees, and tips on motivating contributions from lower-paid employees are from "Pension Plans Pay Off for Small Businesses, Too," *Business Week*, January 29, 1990.

IRS pension audit data is from "IRS Targets Thousands of Small Businesses," *Wall Street Journal*, March 27, 1990.

CHAPTER FOURTEEN

John Davis anecdote, rates for HMO, Blues plan in Maryland are from "On-Your-Own Insurance," *Health*, October 1990.

Ray Porter anecdote, Paul McAvoy quote are from "Disability Insurance: Treat Your Body Like an Oil Well," *Gannett Westchester Newspapers*, January 25, 1988.

Robert Hollomand anecdote is from "Managing the High Cost of Health Care," *Black Enterprise*, October 1988.

Data on own-occ policies from "Disability Insurance," *Money*, 1989.

Keogh participation statistics are from *Fundamentals of Employee Benefit Programs*, Employee Benefit Research Institute, 1990.

The downside to the defined benefit Keogh is from "Retirement Plans," *Consumer Reports*, March 1990.

Steven Enright quote is from "More People Find SEP/IRAs as a Popular Alternative," *Boston Globe*, November 20, 1989.

CHAPTER FIFTEEN

Robert Half quote is from "Hire Smart: the Artful Interview," *Working Woman*, March 1989.

Michael Lonto quote is from "Reference Checks: How to Get the Information You Need," *Working Woman*, May 1989.

Statistics on the cost of providing employee benefits are from Table 4a, "Employee Benefits, by Type of Benefits, All Employees, 1990," *Employee Benefits*, U.S. Chamber Research Center.

CHAPTER SIXTEEN

State-by-state data on health care legislation are from "Small Employer Rating and Renewability Requirements," "Comprehensive Small Employer Packages," and "Limited Mandated Benefits Laws," Health Insurance Association of America.

INDEX